# Emotional Abuse Breakthrough

## How to Speak Up, Set Boundaries, and Break the Cycle of Manipulation and Control with Your Abusive Partner

Barrie Davenport

ISBN: 1537339346
ISBN-13: 9781537339344

# Disclaimer

# Your Free Gift

As a way of saying thank you for your purchase, please begin this book by taking my Emotional Abuse Test to help you clarify if you are in an emotionally abusive relationship. Many people are confused about whether or not certain behaviors qualify as abusive. This assessment covers the specific behaviors and language that emotional abusers use consistently.

You can download your assessment and get your personal score by going to this site:

**http://liveboldandbloom.com/book-test**

# Contents

# About Barrie Davenport

Barrie Davenport is a certified personal coach, thought leader, author, and creator of several online courses on self-confidence, life passion, habit creation, and self-publishing. She is the founder of two top-ranked personal development sites, LiveBoldandBloom.com and BarrieDavenport.com. Her work as a coach, blogger, and author is focused on offering people practical strategies for living happier, more successful, and more mindful lives. She utilizes time-tested, evidence based, action-oriented principles and methods to create real and measurable results for self-improvement.

You can learn more about Barrie on her Amazon author page at barriedavenport.com/author.

x

# Introduction

*"You are very powerful, provided you know how powerful you are."*

—Yogi Bhajan

If you're reading this book, you probably recognize or suspect that you're living with an emotional abuser.

You may be just coming to terms with what's going on with your partner's behavior, or you may have suffered for years, and you're simply at the end of your rope.

What matters is that you don't have to live this way any longer, and you know something has to change. By reading this book, you've taken the first step to implement change, and that's empowering.

When I've coached or talked to clients who've suffered with emotional abuse from their spouse or partner, I hear things like this:

I feel powerless and used.

Why can't he change and show me real love?

Why does she have to be so manipulative and controlling?

I've lost my self-respect.

I feel like a prisoner and I don't know what to do.

I don't know how I'd live without him.

I have to keep the peace for the kids.

It feels like I'm the one who's crazy.

She always turns things around to blame me.

I don't have any options. I'm stuck.

How do I stand up for myself and demand my rights?

I feel like I've been brainwashed.

Is it possible that he could change?

If you can relate to these questions and concerns, you've come to the right place. We will address all of these throughout this book, so you can walk away with more clarity about whether to remain in the relationship or leave it. You'll also have the strategies to reclaim your personal power and self-esteem no matter what you decide.

Every person's situation with an emotional abuser is different, and every abusive relationship has its own dynamics. But all victims have the same goal—to end the abuse and live a happy life. That's what I want for you, and that's what you deserve.

Before we dive in, please be cautioned that if you're experiencing physical abuse or violence, this book is NOT the solution for you. Emotional abuse can lead to physical abuse, and there are three types of emotional abuse that appear to predict physical abuse. These include threats, restriction of your actions, and damage to your property (Diane Follingstad et al., "The Role of Emotional Abuse in Physically Abusive Relationships," 1990).

If you are the victim of physical violence or suspect it could happen, you must seek professional assistance right away for your own safety and the safety of anyone living in the home with you, particularly your children.

Please contact a local abuse hotline, a licensed counselor, or the police as soon as possible. You can also contact the National Domestic Violence Hotline at 1-800-799-SAFE (7233) or for the deaf or hard of hearing, contact 1-800-787-3224 (TTY). Your life really could depend on it.

I'd like to also mention that I'm not a doctor, psychiatrist, or licensed counselor. I'm a professional coach and personal growth teacher who has worked with emotionally abused clients and people suffering with low self-esteem and low confidence.

My work is to help people move forward in their lives wherever they happen to be right now. I firmly believe that positive action is the key to having a better life.

The information presented in this book is thoroughly researched and based on the professional advice and recommendations of various qualified resources.

My job is to facilitate awareness, both of the emotional abuser in your life and of yourself, and to present options for managing your situation, making change when you need to, and healing from the damage that emotional abuse creates.

Here's something you must know from the outset: you can't improve or change your life in an abusive relationship unless you make it happen. The emotional abuser is not going to initiate change on his (or her) own.

Yes, women can be emotional abusers as well as men. Some studies suggest that women and men emotionally abuse each other at equal rates, and emotional abuse can occur in any type of relationship, including parent and child, boss and employee, and friend with friend.

However, this book focuses on intimate love relationships, whether you are a woman or man, gay or straight.

As we begin, I'd like to share a comment from one of my blog readers who is a victim of emotional abuse. Here's what she says:

*I put up with it and put up with it and put up with it. Because I love him and I know his mom abused him and his ex-wife had a string of affairs, he struggles with trust issues. And I thought if I could just prove myself enough, I'd make it all OK, and he'd realize I was honest and loyal and loved him.*

Does this sound familiar? Those who are emotionally abused do put up with it. They often take the blame for the crazy-making behaviors or justify them because the abuser makes them feel guilty or stupid.

The abused partner tries so hard to prove his or her love and loyalty in the hopes that the abuser will finally wake up and connect in a healthy, loving, and mature way. Sadly, unless the abuser is highly motivated to change, this doesn't happen without intervention.

Each person reading this book has a unique set of difficulties and life circumstances affecting their actions and decisions related to their abusive partner. The emotional abuse may be constant and severe, or it might be just enough to make you think it will get better, like the slow drip of water torture.

Through this book, you'll come to better understand and navigate your particular situation to reach the result that works best for your life. You may decide to remain in the relationship, or you may decide to leave it. But either way, you should *never* accept the status quo. You deserve better, and you DON'T have to take it any more. You are more powerful than you think.

# Chapter 1:
# What Is Emotional Abuse?

*"If the wounds on her heart and the bruises on
her soul were translated on her skin,
you wouldn't recognize her at all."*

—Verona Q

Maybe you haven't been hit or pushed or locked in
a closet. There are no physical scars, black eyes,
or bruises on your arms and legs.

You haven't had to wear dark glasses, call the
police, or make a middle-of-the-night trip to the
emergency room. At least not yet.

One of the little-known truths about emotional
abuse is that physical abuse in domestic
relationships is almost always preceded and
accompanied by psychological abuse.

More surprisingly, emotional abuse by one partner
is the most reliable predictor of the other partner's
likelihood of first exhibiting *physical* aggression.
Those who are emotionally abused eventually
crack and want to strike out. Too often they do.

Emotional abuse (also referred to as covert aggression or psychological abuse) shouldn't be taken lightly. It can and often does lead to violence and even death, and it always causes emotional distress to its victims.

If you are in an emotionally abusive relationship, taking action now before you or your partner becomes physically aggressive, is the best thing you can do for yourself and the people you love. The first step is to understand what you're dealing with.

## What Is Emotional Abuse Exactly?

You know what it feels like. You know the conflicted emotions and reactions you have to the comments, looks, and behaviors that leave you feeling isolated, unloved, angry, and afraid.

But why is it so hard to pinpoint this abuse, especially when your partner is so good at denying it or covering it up? How do you quantify the damage when attitudes do the wounding and behaviors leave no physical trace?

According to Andrew Vachss, an author, attorney, and former sex crimes investigator, "Emotional abuse is the systematic diminishment of another. It may be intentional or subconscious (or both), but it is always a course of conduct, not a single event."

Any one isolated comment or behavior exhibited by an emotional abuser could be considered a normal, expected, but infrequent, reaction to relationship conflict or stress. We all say and do things on occasion that are hurtful, passive aggressive, or controlling.

What distinguishes emotional or psychological abuse is the pattern of behavior. As Andrew Vachss says, it is a course of conduct that is systematic. It feels like a form of slow brainwashing.

This definition from Dr. Marti Tamm Loring, a clinical social worker, sociologist, and director of the Center for Mental Health and Human Development and The Emotional Abuse Institute, says it best. "Emotional abuse is an ongoing process in which one individual systematically diminishes and destroys the inner self of another. The essential ideas, feelings, perceptions, and personality characteristics of the victim are constantly belittled" (*Emotional Abuse,* 1994, p. 1).

Emotional abusers can use verbal abuse and constant criticism, as well as more subtle and insidious tactics, such as intimidation, emotional manipulation, passive aggressive and controlling behaviors, and a refusal to ever be pleased.

They use these subtle tactics not only to blind you to their real nature and self-serving agendas, but also to exert their power to bring you to submission and control you.

Says Dr. George Simon, an internationally recognized expert on manipulators, "Dealing with these folks is often like getting whiplash: you only fully realize what's happened to you after most of the damage has been done."

There are three main elements of emotionally abusive behavior: aggression, denying, and minimizing. Abusers try to make you fearful, they deny their behaviors, and they diminish both you and their own roles in the problem.

They become so good at it, they often do it unconsciously, knowing on some level they'll get the desired response. Every time you give them what they want, you reinforce the behavior. When you don't give them what they want, their aggressive or shaming responses make you quickly toe the line.

The impact that emotional abuse has on its victims is profound, as you well know. Blaming, shaming, and name-calling are common forms of verbal abuse, and together emotional and verbal abuse undermine a person's foundational confidence and self-love, and replaces them with deep confusion about worthiness, mutual love, and respect.

Victims of emotional abuse can experience more severe psychological reactions. A victim may feel their emotions are affected to such an extent that he or she no longer recognizes their own true feelings related to issues or situations the abuser is trying to control. As a result, the victim's self-concept, confidence, and independence are systematically broken down.

Here's a heartbreaking example of this situation shared by one of my blog readers:

## Emotional Abuse Breakthrough

*At first I thought, "He is just a perfectionist," or he probably has mild OCD [obsessive-compulsive disorder] when he would tell me to do things a certain way. And he was very polite about it in the beginning. Now no matter what I do, it is not right or good enough.*

*Simple things like loading the dishwasher or cleaning the bathroom. It's the worst if I happen to drop a crumb of food and not search for it, pick it up, and throw it away.*

*I work two jobs, I'm in college fulltime, and manage to do almost all the cooking and cleaning. I even stay up for most of the day just to be able to spend more time with him.*

*But it's never a big deal to him. It's not that hard to him, or he didn't tell me to clean, or didn't tell me to make dinner. But that's not true at all. He doesn't ever demand that I do something, but he loves to guilt-trip me. He calls them "jokes."*

*He constantly says something that I find very rude or sarcastic, and ends it with, "Just kidding, it was a joke." It has gone on for so long that we both refer to these types of jokes as "bad jokes."*

*So when he says something that hurts my feelings, he will say, "Bad joke. Don't get mad." Now he is starting to tell me that I'm too sensitive, and I can't take a joke. He threatens that he just won't joke with me any more, because I don't know him well enough to understand he is just kidding.*

*And it makes me feel awful, so I'm always saying, "I'm sorry, I just wasn't sure if you were being serious or not." I am constantly trying to do nice things for him, or anything that will make him happy. Because those are the only times he will praise me, compliment me, or give me affection.*

You can see how this abuser created a pattern of behavior that was seemingly innocent at first. But it grew more and more manipulative and controlling until the victim was doing backflips trying to appease and please the abuser.

She is stuck in a cycle of despair and pain, trying desperately to gather any crumbs of affection and love from him, while he is playing her like a puppet to get her to do his bidding. As she says, "My biggest fear in life is to be alone," but she doesn't realize she's selling her soul to prevent loneliness.

Emotional abuse is characterized by intent, a power disparity, escalation of behavior, duration, and repetition. It is based in a need for power and control.

The tactics may differ slightly from abuser to abuser, but the results are always the same. Emotional abuse destroys the hope of a real relationship. Trust, intimacy, security, and happiness are impossible in an environment where one partner seeks to dominate, belittle, and intimidate the other.

Now that you understand a little more about emotional abuse, let's talk about how the abuse might be impacting you and your family.

Barrie Davenport

# Chapter 2:
# What's Happening to Me?

*"If I could show you how awful you made me
feel, you would never be able to
look me in the eye again."*

—Unknown

If you've been living with emotional abuse, you've
been scarred. The scars may not be visible to other
people, but you feel them intensely.

The amount of scarring you've experienced will
depend on the severity of the abuse, the length of
time you've experienced it, and on your personal
history and personality. We'll get more into your
history in another chapter, but make no mistake, all
emotional abuse hurts deeply. I'm sure I don't have
to tell you that.

In fact, emotional abuse can be more
psychologically harmful than physical abuse. Even
in the most physically abusive relationships, the
incidents of violence tend to be cyclical.

Barrie Davenport

Early in the cycle of physical abuse, a violent outburst is followed by a honeymoon period of remorse, attention, affection, and generosity, although not often genuine compassion.

Emotional abuse, however, tends to happen every day or several times a week. The effects are more harmful because they're so frequent and insidious.

## Is This Really Abuse?

Many victims of emotional abuse don't see the mistreatment as abusive. A University of Oregon study showed that the victims tend to have more difficulty identifying and processing their own emotions. Also by minimizing the abusive behaviors, victims may be using a coping mechanism to try to tolerate stress or conflict.

One of my blog readers shared her own story of confusion about the abuse in her relationship. She wrote:

> I have been with my fiancé for almost four years. I have read several posts, and still can't decide or pinpoint or be sure he is emotionally abusive even though all the signs are there. The worst part is we just had a kid and live with his parents. It's hard to say if I'm just emotionally overreacting, because he told me to my face he doesn't feel guilty for wanting other people.

Her fiancé has the signs of an emotional abuser and tells her he desires other women, but she's confused about whether or not she's overreacting. This confusion and self-blame is common with victims of emotional abuse.

If you've been in a long-term relationship with an abuser, or if you have never had a healthy, loving romantic relationship, you may assume this combative, manipulative way of relating is what "normal couples do."

You might believe that relationships are naturally difficult and that your partner's behavior is just symptomatic of a typical dynamic between couples. Unfortunately, too many couples do experience emotional abuse in their relationship—but it isn't normal or healthy.

## Self-Blame and Hypervigilance

Another reason emotional abuse is so devastating is the likelihood that victims will blame themselves. If your spouse is hitting you, it's clear that he or she is the problem.

However, when the abuse is subtle, through passive-aggressive behaviors, guilt tripping, manipulation, or blaming, you're more likely to believe it's your problem—or at least you had some hand in it.

Your partner wouldn't be so upset with you if you weren't to blame. Someone who's supposed to love you wouldn't treat you this way if you didn't deserve it.

These are the kind of crazy-making thoughts emotional abuse fosters. It makes love feel confusing, painful, and unpredictable. It seems more personal than physical abuse, more about your essential self and identity.

It also makes you feel emotionally unsafe and insecure. Over time, you may doubt yourself, your opinions, your senses, feelings, memories, beliefs, abilities, and judgment.

As your sense of self is eroded, you might express your opinions less and less freely and find yourself questioning your sense of reality. You may feel vulnerable, unworthy, and increasingly trapped and powerless. This may lead you to become anxious, agitated, and even depressed.

Emotional abuse victims walk on eggshells around their spouse or partner, always hypervigilant and fearful of saying or doing something that could trigger the abuse.

Your words are measured and carefully presented, and you hold back speaking your real feelings or concerns.

You have to be on your best behavior, unable to relax or enjoy the moment because you are consciously or subconsciously fearing the worst. Even when your spouse is being "good," you are always anticipating the other side to be displayed at any moment.

It's not uncommon for emotionally abused partners to feel responsible for fixing their loved one's bad mood, immature behaviors, or abusive actions.

You become attached to magical thinking, hoping things will change if only you could get through to them or change your behavior just so. If you just loved him more, showed him more care and understanding, he'll come around and stop acting so horrible. This only reinforces the abuser's control over you.

Victims of abuse long for the kind, caring side of their partners to reappear, knowing it's there somewhere inside of them because it's been evident in the past. You long for the return of the person you first met and fell in love with.

We ALL deeply desire and inherently require love, affection, warmth, and kindness, but when you're only getting the crumbs from the table, even the crumbs begin to feel like manna from heaven.

You think that a morsel of love and attention is better than nothing at all. So to collect that morsel, you find yourself making excuses for your partner's bad behavior. You try desperately to get him or her back into the previous good behavior state.

## Traumatic Bonding

Another counterintuitive characteristic of emotional abuse is something called traumatic bonding. This is when you create a strong emotional attachment with your abusive partner, and the bond strengthens the more you experience the abuse and trauma.

This bonding is why so many abuse victims proclaim their strong love for their abuser. They are mistaking traumatic bonding with love.

With loss of power in the relationship, the victim's sense of self as a valuable person starts to disintegrate, and he or she becomes more dependent on the abusive partner. The more dependent the victim becomes, the more he or she will cling to the abuser and put up with the abusive behaviors because of abandonment anxiety.

This is similar to Stockholm syndrome, which is common in long-term, severe abuse situations. Here the victim is so terrified of the abuser that the victim overly identifies with the abuser and bonds with him or her in an attempt to end the abuse. Sometimes the victim will even defend the abuser and the destructive, cruel actions.

## The Fallout

Depending on your particular relationship and the length of time the abuse has been going on, you'll experience short-term and/or long-term effects of the abuse.

You will recognize many of these feelings and behaviors in yourself, and knowing you have them may feel painful and scary. But this self-awareness is an important step toward reclaiming your life.

Take a deep breath, and let's look at some of the emotional fallout created by the abuser in your life.

Short-term effects generally relate to the shock and surprise of landing in the abusive relationship and questioning how the situation arose. Some abusive partners are kind and loving during the courtship and early relationship months, but then the abuse appears later on.

The victim may be taken off guard and shocked to see the new, emotionally abusive behavior. As the abuse continues and intensifies, the victim's behavior and thoughts also change in response to the emotional abuse.

You may have an intense need to draw closer to the abuser to understand the abuse and seek to resolve it.

## These are some of the short-term effects of emotional abuse:

- Feeling surprise and confusion.
- Feeling misunderstood and defensive.
- Feeling desperate, overly needy; requiring constant reassurance.
- Questioning yourself and your memory.
- Experiencing anxiety, agitation, or fear; hypervigilance.
- Experiencing shame, embarrassment, or guilt.
- Acting out with aggression (as a defense to the abuse).
- Becoming overly passive or compliant.

- Crying frequently.
- Avoiding eye contact.
- Feeling powerless, helpless, and defeated.
- Monitoring your own behaviors and words.
- Feeling manipulated, betrayed, used, and controlled.
- Feeling undesirable.

At this stage, the victim may try to do anything possible to restore the relationship to the way it was before the abuse.

If this is where you are in the cycle of emotional abuse, you don't have to let this spiral further out of control. Before you are further debilitated, recognize what you are dealing with here and that it's not your fault. You AREN'T crazy or helpless.

You do have power over yourself, despite what your abuser may tell you. We'll get into claiming your power later in the book. For now, simply accept the truth. You are living with an emotional abuser, but at this early stage the situation isn't hopeless.

This is the best time to alter the trajectory of your relationship before you lose more power and self-esteem.

Unfortunately, many victims are too confused and fearful to take action during the earlier stages of emotional abuse. They try to cobble together a tolerable existence, feeding off the occasional periods of normalcy or kindness from their partner.

Maybe they find fulfillment and joy through other outlets, such as work, children, and hobbies. But because of the dynamic of the intimate relationship and the control the abuser exerts on his or her partner, it's impossible to escape the damaging effects of this behavior over the long term. The victim is slowly worn down until there's barely anything left.

When an emotionally abusive relationship has been going on for many years, the victim's self-esteem has hit rock bottom. It can be so low that victims often feel they can't leave their abuser and may believe they aren't worthy of a nonabusive relationship.

The victim begins to believe the terrible things the abuser says about him or her. At this point many abuse victims think they're "going crazy" because they have lost their sense of self. If the couple has children, the victims find it even harder to pull away, as they feel responsible for keeping the peace at all costs for the well-being and protection of the children.

You must recognize that children who witness the emotional abuse of a parent are being emotionally abused themselves. Seeing one parent berate, stonewall, diminish, or verbally attack the other is extremely painful and confusing for the child.

Witnessing this on a regular basis has long-term negative consequences on the child's emotional development. If the adult victim of emotional abuse can't comprehend the destructive, confusing behaviors of the abuser, you can only imagine the inner world of the child who is witnessing it.

The child grows up believing a committed relationship involves one partner who controls and manipulates and another who is helpless. As we'll discuss later, this can be the beginning of a cycle of abuse that spans generations.

Women who are homemakers, stay-at-home moms, and who don't work outside the home, are often trapped in an untenable situation. The abusive spouse controls the finances and is the only wage earner.

Without another means of support, no easy access to money, and the pressure to ensure their children's welfare, these women feel completely hopeless. Eventually hopelessness turns to despair, and serious mental and physical illness can be the result.

This kind of hopeless is by no means exclusive to women. Men who are emotionally abused feel equally handcuffed and despairing, wanting to protect children, maintain financial stability, and save the relationship if at all possible.

Both women and men remain in emotionally abusive relationships with the best intentions. They love their partners and hope things will somehow get better. They want to protect their children and maintain the integrity of the family. Unfortunately, the effects of long-term emotional abuse make it much more difficult to take action and stop the abuse.

## Here are some of the long-term effects of emotional abuse:

- Depression
- Generalized anxiety
- Panic attacks
- Withdrawal
- Low self-esteem and low self-worth
- Emotional instability
- Sleep disturbances
- Unexplained physical pain
- Suicidal thoughts or attempts
- Extreme dependence on the abuser
- Underachievement
- Inability to trust
- Feeling trapped and alone
- Substance abuse

If you've been in an abusive relationship for many years, you may be suffering with some of these effects. These are not issues to take lightly. Depression, anxiety, emotional instability, suicidal thoughts, and substance abuse can lead to serious mental and/or physical health problems or even death.

It's hard to be a good parent, employee, or friend when you are just holding on by a thread. You may not have the wherewithal right now to challenge or change your relationship, but you DO need to protect yourself from further psychological damage.

I'll go over various coping strategies later in the book, but for now, I'd like to encourage you to find a support outlet, especially if you're dealing with depression. You need to talk with someone, and the best person is a trained professional therapist and/or psychiatrist. Start treating your depression, so you have the mental and emotional energy to handle the rest of your life and to deal with this abusive relationship.

There's no question that emotional abuse has a negative impact on you and your children, if you have them. That's why you're reading this book and seeking answers and relief from this confusing nightmare. To help you better understand why this is happening to you, it's valuable to learn more about the mind of the abuser and some of the patterns of emotional abuse you might recognize.

# Chapter 3:
# The Patterns of
# Emotional Abuse

*"Sometimes we refuse to see
how bad something is
until it completely destroys us."*

—Unknown

Emotional abuse is one of the most pervasive but least recognized kinds of abuse. It can be as damaging as physical or sexual abuse and crosses all social classes, ethnic groups, sexual orientations, and religions. The common denominators of abusers are not demographic but rather personal, social, and psychological.

The abuser in your life may be attentive and kind in public, but once you're alone, the nasty behaviors and attitudes appear like clockwork. He or she might wait until you are in front of family and friends, and then start to make a scene so you'll quickly back down or comply.

You have become the emotional punching bag for your partner's criticism, anger, put-downs, and cold shoulder. The abuse can erupt over just about anything, from matters large to small, such as housework, friends, cooking, work, spending money, children, and going out.

As a result of your loss of self-esteem and your abuser's denials, you may be confused about whether or not the attitudes and actions of your spouse or partner really qualify as emotional abuse. The fact that you are reading this book suggests that they do. But let's examine some of the specific patterns and behaviors to help you gain clarity.

To be abusive, the words and behaviors can't be isolated or infrequent. It must be behavior that's more the norm than the exception. The qualifiers for emotional abuse include *consistency*, *repetition*, *duration*, and *intention*.

The intention of control and hurt behind the anger is what jettisons the behavior into abusive anger that must be confronted and stopped.

There are emotional abusers who may be unaware that some of their behaviors or words are abusive. For example, someone whose parents were emotionally abusive may be repeating the behaviors they learned as children.

However, this lack of awareness doesn't make it any less painful or destructive for the victims. Even if the abusers aren't completely aware, they must notice the impact they are having on you. Please don't use your abuser's past as a way to diminish his or her behavior.

You'll find that abusive behaviors often fall into certain patterns or categories that are persistent and clear. Your partner may exhibit behaviors from one specific category or across several of them.

## Here are the patterns you may recognize:

### Domination

Domination happens when the abuser attempts to control you, your behavior, and even your thoughts and beliefs. The abuser has a need to always have his or her own way and resorts to threats, possessiveness, restriction, and isolation to do so.

### Verbal Assaults

The abuser uses angry, threatening, belittling, humiliating, shaming, blaming, critical, or sarcastic language to control you and hurt you.

Verbal abuse can take more subtle forms, such as making "jokes" that are meant to wound.

Abusers can use a quiet voice to wound, but often they resort to yelling and screaming, which is both hurtful and frightening, especially to children in the family who might overhear.

### Demanding Expectations

Your partner has constant expectations that you meet his or her demands, and yet the partner is never satisfied because there's always something more you could have done.

They insist you meet their needs and put aside your own to do so. They may want your undivided attention, require you to jump up to serve them, or insist on sex when it suits them.

## Emotional Blackmail

Emotional blackmail is yet another way of the abusive partner getting his or her way, but it is far more calculating than just making a verbal demand.

Your partner manipulates you through fear, guilt, shame, or fake compassion to get what they want. They might say something like, "If you really love me, you wouldn't spend the evening with the guys tonight," or "If you invite your parents over, I'm taking the kids and leaving the house."

Emotional blackmail can also include withholding affection, kindness, or sex until the abusive partner gets his or her way. Even giving you the cold shoulder or freezing you out is a subtle form of emotional blackmail.

## Unpredictable Behavior

Emotional abuse can take the form of crazy-making behavior. One minute, she's kind and loving, and the next, she's giving you the cold shoulder.

In the morning he's calm, but in a few hours he's yelling at you for no apparent reason. What makes your spouse angry one day may not bother him or her the next.

This isn't a one-off situation but a pattern of off-kilter behaviors that make you feel insecure and unsettled at best and sometimes downright frightened. You're constantly on edge, waiting for the other shoe to drop. It's like living with Dr. Jekyll and Mr. Hyde, two conflicting sides of the same person.

## Chaos and Crisis Creation

Your partner isn't happy unless he or she is stirring the pot or creating upheaval. He may intentionally start an argument with you or someone in your circle of friends.

She might thrive off the drama and excitement of seeing everyone around her react—particularly you.

The abuser seems to exist in a cloud of chaos which he or she keeps stirred up constantly.

## Character Assassination

Your abuser wants to put you down and humiliate or embarrass you in front of other people. He or she might undermine your achievements, or talk about you behind your back, lie to others about you, or try to harm your reputation.

Your partner might try to disguise this as humor, and perhaps others think it's a lighthearted jab, but you and your abuser know better.

## Gaslighting

This term originates from the 1944 movie called *Gaslight,* in which the husband subtly tries to make his wife doubt her perceptions.

When your partner gaslights you, he or she might deny something that you both know is true or pretend something happened that really didn't.

He or she might suggest you're lying or exaggerating in an attempt to make you feel stupid or crazy. This is a way to control you or for the abuser to shirk responsibility for his or her actions.

## Sexual Harassment

If your partner tries to force you through words or actions to engage in sexual activity against your will, this is a form of harassment and abuse.

Or if your partner tries to force you (through threats, insults, guilt trips, etc.) to engage in sexual acts that you don't feel comfortable with, this is also sexual harassment.

At the end of this book, I've include a list of specific behaviors that fall into each of these categories to help you identify the abusive behaviors in your relationship.

It's important to view these various behaviors on a continuum. On the one end are the occasional hurtful behaviors that can occur in any relationship, such as withdrawing momentarily, listening without empathy, or speaking sharply in anger.

On the more harmful end of the continuum is the pervasive, one-sided, severe psychological control that can parallel intentional brainwashing and torment.

However, any relationship that involves consistent words and behaviors to control and manipulate another person must be considered maladaptive and abusive. The more severe the behaviors, the more psychological and emotional damage the victim experiences.

As your partner trains you behave in ways that he or she desires, he gradually makes you feel differently about yourself, eroding your self-esteem and trust in yourself.

Quite often the abuser's continuous and unrelenting pattern of emotional abuse is interspersed with some warmth and kindness. This fosters a sense of hope in the victim that the behaviors may change, but it also builds a desperate kind of bonding feeling in the victim.

You doubt whether you are really perceiving what you think you're perceiving. If he or she can be so nice, can they also be so cruel and controlling? Maybe it's just you. Maybe your perceptions are skewed.

Please don't be fooled by this. Being fed crumbs of kindness and affection doesn't mean abuse isn't present and that you aren't legitimately suffering.

Nor does occasional good behavior negate the hostile intentions of your spouse or partner.

33

Consistent abusive behavior, even if it's interspersed with occasional kindness, is damaging and destructive.

If you haven't yet taken the Emotional Abuse Test (http://liveboldandbloom.com/emotional-abuse-test) mentioned at the front of this book, now is a good time to take the test to help you feel more clarity about your relationship.

# Chapter 4:
# The Dynamics of Emotionally Abusive Relationships

*"An emotionally abusive relationship,
in very simplistic terms, is much like
standing up in a too hot bath and
sinking back in so as not to feel so dizzy."*

—Jackie Haze

Emotional abuse is a form of long-term mental torture, and when it's inflicted by the one person who is nearest and dearest to you, it is a grievous betrayal of trust and the sledgehammer than shatters your hopes and dreams.

There are many variations of an emotionally abusive relationship, and the dynamics between every couple can escalate and change throughout the years.

A common dynamic of emotional abuse is the relationship in which one partner is abusive and the other one is not. You live with the aggression for a variety of reasons. You're scared of leaving, you feel you have no options, or you still love your spouse and don't want to leave him or her.

Maybe you've become so accustomed to the maliciousness and lack of respect that it feels "normal." You may not trust your own judgment, feelings, and values because your partner has made you feel crazy and confused, especially if he or she never takes any responsibility for the problems in the relationship.

You have lost any power in the relationship, and you spend too much time walking on eggshells, trying to manage what you say and do, so your abuser won't erupt.

## The Aggression Cycle

It's not surprising that emotional abuse from one partner can have the unfortunate side effect of fostering aggression in you as the abused partner.

Even if your partner initiated and reinforces his or her abusive behaviors, your fear and confusion can transform into anger, envy, violence, rage, and hatred.

Abuse fosters abuse, and just as your abuser may have suffered from childhood abuse, you may become just one more cog in the cycle, as you act out your own pain and frustrations. You may internalize your pain in the form of anxiety and depression, or you can externalize it through overt or passive aggression.

The hurtful and confusing behaviors inflicted on you by your partner can transform you into someone you don't recognize and certainly never intended to be.

Because of your abuser's relentless control and manipulation, you feel like an alien life form has invaded your mind and taken up permanent residence. You can be infected by the abuse and engage in an ongoing struggle of hurt, recrimination, denial, and other dysfunctional behaviors.

## Taking Revenge

When your spouse creates a pattern of emotional abuse, you begin reciprocating as a way of self-defense or venting your extreme feelings of pain and confusion. This can happen immediately or even after a few years of tolerating the abuse.

When you've tried everything possible to please your partner, but all you get back is disapproval, emotional coldness, and rejection, then you may start slinging humiliating words and insults toward your partner.

This is exactly what happened to one of my readers, but her anger and retribution grew out of control. Here's what she shared about her experience:

> *Rather than leave, which is what I needed to do, I got angry. Really angry. And so in the past six months I've smashed up the*

37

*bedroom, I've hit him four times, I've thrown
a drink in his face, and I've had my hands
around his throat.*

*Each time it was when he was saying yet
another thing about me sleeping with
someone else, and I just saw red. But I am
now a physical abuser, and I hate myself.*

*He has ended the relationship because I am
a physical abuser and told everyone that
I've been abusing him, which is true, I have.
I know that I wouldn't have hurt him if I
wasn't at the end of my tether, but all
abusers blame their victims.*

So am I suggesting that emotional abuse victims
are abusers themselves? No, not exactly. Self-
defense is never the same as initiating abuse.

Your aggressive responses come from a feeling
that you have to protect yourself and from extreme
feelings of frustration and pent-up anger. Because
hostility seems to be the only form of
communication an abuser understands, it's hard
not to resort to the same type of behavior yourself.
Maybe then your abuser will get a taste of his own
medicine and see how it feels to be treated in such
demeaning ways.

But fighting fire with fire rarely has the desired
outcome. It may make you feel better in the short
term, but in the long run it only continues the cycle
of abuse. It can add to your own feelings of guilt,
shame, and confusion, making it even harder for
you to address the problems with your partner. It

can also give your abuser ammunition to turn the tables and claim you are the abuser.

Even covert retaliation and passive-aggressive behaviors, such as spending money without telling your spouse or undermining your partner to your children, can backfire on you and make you feel more victimized and manipulated.

If you find yourself acting out with abusive language or behaviors, you need to do everything you can to stop. This escalation of the aggression in your household can lead to physical violence and cause further psychological damage to your children.

You may feel completely overwhelmed by your desire to take revenge, and if that's the case, you need the immediate intervention of a counselor who can help you create a plan for dealing with your emotions.

## Progressive Mutual Abuse

A different form of abusive dynamic occurs when the two partners progressively abuse each other from the beginning of the relationship.

Both partners accept the unhealthy, damaging behaviors, and they are doled out in equal measure by each person. One partner may have started it, but enough time has elapsed that now both are equally abusive.

Barrie Davenport

Beverly Engel, the author of *The Emotionally Abusive Relationship*, suggests that this mutual abuse is characterized by these actions:

- Using sarcasm, critiques, and sharp comments.

- Reproaching each other for failures and mistakes from the past.

- Blaming each other for life and relationship problems.

- Attempting to make the other jealous by flirting or by saying how attractive someone else is.

- Complaining frequently about the other partner's behavior.

- Punishing each other with indifference and emotional coldness.

- Competing between themselves to prove who's the smartest, who's the most accomplished, etc.

- Preying on the other partner's helplessness and insecurity.

- Attempting to isolate each other from family and friends.

This kind of relationship can occur when retaliation gets out of hand, or when the victim simply learns to mimic the behaviors of the initial abuser. It becomes a power struggle that never ends.

A 2007 study of Spanish college students between the ages of 18–27 found that emotional abuse is so widespread in dating relationships that it's seen as a normal part of dating. The study also found that women are substantially more likely to exhibit psychological aggression.

## Turning the Table on the Victim

In some emotionally abusive relationships, it's hard to discern who's abusing whom because of the subtle and manipulative nature of the abuser's tactics.

Sometimes an abusive spouse intentionally tries to deceive his partner and others by disguising his manipulations and control with kindness or self-pity. This causes the other partner to doubt his or her own perceptions and mental health.

One of my readers had a husband who was a master at hiding his abusive behaviors. She wrote:

> *I'm 69 and now ending a 26-year marriage. I feel so alone. Everyone sides with my husband and no one ever asks me why I left. It wouldn't matter, no one would believe me. Not even my priest speaks to me.*
>
> *My husband is always so good, kind, and wonderful to everyone else but me. In private, he is another person and can go for*

*weeks without acknowledging my presence or speaking to me. I am invisible. I am like a speck of dust on the tip of a pin. I am worthless.*

My reader's sense of self-worth was not only crushed in her marriage, but also her husband deceived others into believing she was at fault, leaving her feeling isolated and hopeless. He hurt her, abandoned her, and then made sure others saw *him* as the victim.

If your abuser was emotionally abused in childhood, particularly if he or she was rejected or abandoned, physically or emotionally, by one or both parents, they will be extremely sensitive to any kind of rejection from other people.

If they were excessively controlled or emotionally suffocated by their parents or in a previous relationship, then it's likely they'll be sensitive to any form of control from you, even though they are also controlling.

Even the simplest commitment can be emotionally suffocating, so they need to constantly create chaos in their relationships to feel free and in control of their lives.

A frequent result of repeated emotional abuse is hypersensitivity. If you or your partner have been emotionally abused in the past, you may have developed the sense that any kind of comment or action from the outside feels negative and critical. When you've been criticized, disapproved of, and negatively judged, you tend to act accordingly.

In some dysfunctional and emotionally abusive relationships, one partner will intentionally try to goad the other to lose control and exhibit abusive behavior.

Your abusive partner might say something like, "You don't have the courage to walk out," or "You're not man enough to even stand up for yourself." At some point, you, the victim, crack and reciprocate. Then the initial abuser has the upper hand and can call you out as the abusive one.

## Two Abusive Personalities

In some cases, two abusive and aggressive personality types will pair up, and the result is far from anything that resembles a healthy, happy relationship. Both partners are too busy insulting, manipulating, and attempting to control the other.

It's a real *War of the Roses,* in which both partners only see their own needs and goals and are blinded to their partner's. The abuse poisons the relationship and kills it with contempt and hostility.

When partners abuse each other, it takes a toll on both people, leaving them little energy to manage the daily tasks of their lives. They each lose self-esteem and therefore cling to the relationship to feel more in control. This pattern creates a destructive cycle, as each partner becomes more and more dependent on the other, while both continue to abuse each other.

Says Beverly Engel, "Whether it is one or both partners who are being emotionally abusive, the relationship becomes increasingly more toxic as time goes by. In this polluted environment it is difficult for love not only to grow but to survive" (*The Emotionally Abusive Relationship,* p. 13).

Understanding the type of interaction you have with your abusive partner is key to your self-healing. It's painful to see how abusive behavior has impacted you, particularly if it's transformed your otherwise kind and loving nature into an angry, resentful, and controlling person.

If this is the case, you can't continue to rationalize or justify your behavior because of the treatment you're receiving from your spouse or partner. Acknowledge your own abusive behaviors and recognize that your responses are not healthy or productive. They may be your way of protecting yourself from the pain of abuse, but these behaviors don't end the cycle.

You must be the one to break the cycle of abuse, starting with yourself. You may not have control of how your partner behaves, but you can control your own behaviors. We'll talk more about how to do that later in the book.

# Chapter 5:
# Why Does He or She
# Act This Way?

*"An abuser can seem emotionally needy.
You can get caught in a trap of catering to him,
trying to fill a bottomless pit.
But he's not so much needy as entitled,
so no matter how much you give him,
it will never be enough."*

—Lundy Bancroft

If you're in an emotionally abusive relationship, I'm sure you've wondered many times, "Why does he (or she) do that?" "What's wrong with my partner?"

Although you may blame yourself for some of your spouse's behaviors, or you may try to diminish the abuse, some part of you knows this is not the way a loving spouse or partner should treat you.

And some part of you knows you haven't done anything to deserve the kind of treatment you're getting from this person who is supposed to love, honor, and respect you.

So if you aren't the cause (and you aren't), why then is your partner behaving this way?

Unfortunately, there isn't one simple answer that provides a blanket reason. Although it's important to educate yourself and try to have a better understanding of your partner's inner world, you may not find the complete answer you're looking for.

Every situation is different, and every abuser has a particular temperament, comes from a different background, and has a unique set of life experiences, all of which contribute to the abusive behavior choices.

Sam Vaknin, the author of the book *Malignant Self-Love*, says, "The abuser may be functional or dysfunctional, a pillar of society, or a peripatetic con-artist, rich or poor, young or old. There is no universally-applicable profile of the 'typical abuser'."

I want to clarify that whatever reason your abuser may have for his or her behaviors, no reason justifies the abuse. Emotional abuse is harmful, and on some level all abusers know their behavior is wrong.

The purpose of understanding the mind of an abuser is not to excuse the actions but rather to help you understand and embrace that you are not responsible for the behaviors inflicted on you, even if your abuser was the past victim of abuse.

In fact, some emotional abusers learned to abuse from watching their own parents. In a recent survey of 300 of my blog readers who are victims of emotional abuse, more than 45 percent reported their abuser was emotionally or physically abused or neglected as a child.

If they were abused themselves as children, or if they witnessed one parent abusing the other or abusing a sibling, then they view emotional abuse as the normal condition of life.

If this is the case for your partner, he or she has internalized this abuser/victim relationship dynamic to the extent that it is normalized in their own minds.

Many of my readers who shared their stories of emotional abuse have referred to their partners' childhoods as the reason for their behavior.

"He blames his unstable childhood," says Tonya.

"I felt bad for my husband because of his crappy childhood," says another reader.

"He had a hard childhood; he's been hurt in the past," says yet another victim of abuse.

One admitted emotional abuser commented, "I was mentally and physically abused most of my childhood."

Having suffered the terror of being a helpless victim from their own childhood experience, your partner may have determined never to be a victim again.

But for him or her, the opposite of being a victim is not simply escaping the abuse but rather to be abusive. Given the choice between living as the out-of-control victim or the in-control abuser, your partner may have chosen the latter.

As they become adults and form intimate relationships themselves, emotional abusers simply turn the dynamic around from childhood and start acting out the "abuser" side they know so well from Mom and Dad's interactions.

By choosing to be the aggressor in your relationship, your partner may get his or her first sense of control over their own lives rather than being at the mercy of others. The fact that they are hurting you and your kids in the process may go unregistered or only occur as a dim part of their awareness.

Lundy Bancroft is one of the world's foremost experts on domestic abuse, a former codirector at Emerge, the nation's first program for abusive men, and the author of *Why Does He Do That? Inside the Minds of Angry and Controlling Men*. He believes men abuse for a variety of reasons.

Says Bancroft,
> *Abusiveness has little to do with psychological problems and everything to do with values and beliefs. Where do a boy's values about partner relationships come from? The sources are many. The most important ones include the family he grows up in, his neighborhood, the television he watches and books he reads,*

*jokes he hears, messages that he receives
from the toys he is given, and his most
influential adult role models. His role models
are important not just for which behaviors
they exhibit to the boy but also for which
values they teach him in words and what
expectations they instill in him for the future.
In sum, a boy's values develop from the full
range of his experiences within his* culture
(p. 319).

## Abuse and Personality Disorders

Does your gut tell you there's something "off" with
your abusing partner? Maybe you have the sense
that his or her behavior is not just abusive, it's
abnormal and sick. You may be onto something,
but you just can't put your finger on it.

Emotionally abusive behavior can be tied to mental
health problems or disorders. Both male and
female abusers have higher rates of personality
disorders, such as borderline personality disorder,
narcissistic personality disorder, and antisocial
personality disorder.

Personality disorders are deeply ingrained,
maladaptive patterns of behavior that typically
manifest by the time one reaches adolescence.
These disorders cause long-term difficulties in
personal relationships and often with functioning in
society in general.

In the general population, the rates of these
disorders are roughly 15–20 percent. However, as

a point of reference, 80 percent of abusive men in court-ordered treatment programs have personality disorders (source: https://en.wikipedia.org/wiki/Psychological_abuse).

Just to clarify, simply because your spouse or partner is emotionally abusive doesn't necessarily mean he or she has a personality disorder. But it is quite common for someone with a personality disorder to exhibit emotionally abusive behaviors in their intimate relationships.

These disorders lie on a continuum, and depending on the particular day or moment, your partner may exhibit different characteristics of these disorders.

If you suspect your intimate partner has one of these disorders, don't make the diagnosis on your own. Discuss your partner's symptoms and behaviors with a qualified psychologist or psychiatrist. If possible, ask your partner to join you in talking with a professional, so a clinical diagnosis can be made.

Don't suggest to your partner that you suspect he or she has a personality disorder without having a professional diagnosis made. This could only make the abusive treatment worse for you if your partner feels you are attacking him or her or unfairly characterizing their behavior.

Also, if your partner has anger management issues, a diagnosis of intermittent explosive disorder (explosive outbursts of anger or rage disproportionate to the situation), or if they have a drinking or drug problem, they're much more likely to get out of control during arguments—or even suddenly for no apparent reason.

Their inhibitions are weakened at a brain level, so they feel more free to verbally or psychologically strike out at their partners.

## Lack of Empathy

Some emotional abusers simply have an empathy deficit. They simply can't connect to your feelings. If they were abused themselves as children, their innate empathic abilities never developed properly.

Without the ability to be empathetic, your partner can't or won't relate to you as a person deserving of kindness and respect. Instead, he or she treats you as an object—they confuse people for things, and treat people (namely you) like your sole purpose is for their convenience. Your abuser doesn't view you as having an independent, important life.

Abusers who lack empathy and treat people as objects are likely to be psychologically ill. They may have an antisocial or narcissistic personality disorder, and they may also have anger or impulse control issues and substance abuse issues.

If your abuser lacks empathy, he or she may feel some satisfaction from abusing, like sexual or financial gratification, or the feeling of power over your life.

# Societal Expectations and Roles

For male abusers, the reason for their abuse may relate to religious, ethnic, or patriarchal views about the roles of men and women in relationships.

The abuser may hold the view that men are superior to woman and that it's acceptable to dominate, shame, or control their partner. They may see themselves as the "man of the house," the person in charge who can tell the woman what to do and how to behave.

Your partner's sense of masculinity may depend on your dependency on him. He may feel like a man only when you are totally submissive and dependent on him.

Awareness and acceptance of women's rights has certainly grown during the past few decades, and, as a result, abuse by men is increasingly frowned on and viewed as unacceptable. Most men know that abuse is wrong.

However, there are huge pockets of patriarchal abuse that cut across all demographic and social-economic categories. The truth is, women are physically weaker and, despite recent strides in equal rights, they are still economically restricted.

These facts make women perfect victims for emotional abuse—dependent, helpless, and devalued. Even in the most advanced societies, wives are still expected to serve their husbands, maintain the family and home, give up their autonomy, and ignore their own choices and preferences in favor of their spouse's.

Therefore, the abusing husband believes he's entirely within his rights to impose his whims and decisions on his wife and often children also.

As I mentioned earlier, men are not the only emotional abusers in relationships. Women can exert the same manipulative, controlling behaviors with their nonabusive partners. A woman who has suffered abuse from her partner can become an abuser herself.

Whether your abuser is a man or a woman, all emotional abusers tend to believe they are "owed" by everyone and thus everyone (including their victim) should give them what they want.

This makes them feel entitled to give orders, control, and abuse to bend others to their whims. Similarly, emotionally abusive people tend to be self-centered to the point where they feel they can, and should, tell others how to think and feel.

## Low Self-Esteem

Ironically, emotional abusers often suffer the same low self-esteem and lack of confidence that the victims feel. This lack of self-esteem makes the abusers vulnerable to criticism, disagreement, exposure, and adversity, either real or imagined. As a result, they strike out or control to shore up their self-worth.

Barrie Davenport

Emotional abuse is bred by the fear of being mocked, belittled, or betrayed, as well as emotional insecurity and anxiety. The abuse becomes a last-ditch effort to exert control over you by possessing and punishing you for being a separate being, with your own boundaries, needs, feelings, preferences, and desires.

I think this quote from Dr. Sam Vaknin really says it all about emotional abusers and their relationship with their partners:

> Independent or disobedient people evoke in the abuser the realization that something is wrong with his worldview, that he is not the centre of the world or its cause and that he cannot control what, to him, are internal representations.
>
> To the abuser, losing control means going insane. Because other people are mere elements in the abuser's mind—being unable to manipulate them literally means losing it (his mind).

As you learn more about the possible reasons your partner behaves the way he or she does, remember that these reasons do not justify or excuse the behaviors.

Your spouse or partner is an adult and intellectually knows—or should know—the difference between right and wrong behavior. Even if they are suffering from a personality disorder or mental illness, you don't need to accept their abuse as a result. The abuser's lack of awareness or empathy is not a good reason for allowing it to continue.

Barrie Davenport

# Chapter 6:
# Why You Have an
# Abuser in Your Life

*"All she ever wanted was unpredictable kisses and unforgettable laughter."*

—Brandon Villasenor

If you're stuck in an emotionally abusive relationship, you probably wonder how the heck you wound up in this situation. No one intentionally chooses an abusive partner or consciously seeks out someone who is going to control, wound, and manipulate them.

Part of the crazy-making emotions you experience are the feelings of confusion and shame. How did things get to this point? Why did I allow myself to be in this situation?

I'd like to make it clear that this is not your fault and you are not crazy, gullible, or a poor judge of character. You don't deserve this treatment, and it certainly isn't acceptable, especially in a relationship with an intimate partner who is supposed to love and respect you.

The reasons you are here in an abusive relationship are complicated and complex. They involve both your personal history and life experiences, as well as your partner's.

Beyond these life experiences, neither of you have learned how to establish a healthy and satisfying relationship. If you do understand how a real relationship should operate, you don't have the emotional skills, confidence, and self-awareness to create one in this relationship.

## Childhood Experiences

There are unconscious needs and fears you both act out in the dynamic between you, and these needs and fears often go back to your childhood experiences with your own parents.

Both of you may have experienced or witnessed some kind of abuse or neglect when you were young, and you are responding to this early abuse with coping mechanisms you learned along the way. In the survey I conducted with 300 of my blog readers who are or were victims of emotional abuse, more than 60 percent stated they were the victims of physical or emotional abuse or neglect in their childhoods.

If your first reaction to this news is, "That's not true for me, I wasn't abused as a child," I invite you to reconsider what child abuse and neglect really is.

What you might have considered normal or expected behavior from your parents may well have been abusive or neglectful. Few people who were NOT abused as children would put up with emotional abuse from their intimate partner as an adult.

When you know what healthy, loving, and secure relationships look like, you have the skills to recognize when someone's behavior falls short of that, and you steer clear or demand immediate change.

In a later chapter, we'll talk about some of the specific types of abuse you and your partner may have encountered as children and how this abuse has impacted your choice in partners.

For now, I want you to understand how your childhood experiences may have shaped who you are and how you became a victim of abuse—and how your partner became an abuser.

Certainly there are abusive relationships in which neither partner suffered abuse or neglect as children or young adults. A woman or man who is confident, intelligent, and generally happy can get involved with an abuser.

Abusers are adept at showing a different face at the beginning of a relationship. They can be charming, attentive, and kind, only to slowly reveal their controlling, aggressive, and manipulative true colors. By the time you figure it out, you are entrenched in the relationship and thrown off balance by his or her confusing behaviors.

Those who have never suffered from childhood abuse still have times of vulnerability and low confidence. This is the perfect time for abusers to strike and for you to fall for their ploys.

Their confidence, charm, and attentiveness seem the perfect antidote for your stress and pain. These qualities in a potential love interest are intoxicating for anyone, but especially so for someone who is vulnerable.

## The Biology Factor

Despite strides made in equalizing gender roles, men and women are culturally trained to react differently to fear and pain. Biology certainly has something to do with how we react, but cultural expectations have inevitably shaped us.

In general, men are discouraged from expressing their pain and fear with tears and words, but are given tacit permission to show anger and control.

On the other hand, women are given permission to cry and show emotion, except when it comes to anger. Women are more inclined to repress and suppress angry feelings and internalize their pain.

This isn't true in all cases. There are certainly men who internalize anger and women who express it. But, in general, this is a pattern you see reflected quite often with men and women.

When men are hurt, their instinct is usually to retaliate. They'll strike out with words, attitudes, or actions to protect themselves from further pain. Women, however, are not so quick to retaliate and instead seek to avoid anger and foster peace. In fact, some researchers believe women are biologically wired to work toward peaceful resolutions, even at their own expense.

More important, if something goes awry in a man's world, he's more likely to look outside himself for the cause of the problem. Men are also biologically wired, but for action rather than introspection. They tend to blame others and have a more difficult time taking responsibility for their actions and feelings.

The first place a woman goes when conflict occurs is inside herself. She spends a lot of time internalizing a problem and will often question and blame herself rather than someone else.

This means a woman is more likely to give in during an argument to maintain or restore peace. She is also more likely to feel confused about herself and her role in the conflict. As a result, she often compromises or backs down in the relationship when she shouldn't.

When you internalize anger, back down, and compromise yourself too often, you become resentful and depressed. As time goes on, your self-esteem is severely diminished, which ironically makes you more dependent on the person causing your pain.

You fear abandonment, so you don't want to do anything, like assert yourself or stand up for your opinions, that could jeopardize your relationship and lead to rejection by your partner.

Men often put on an air of indifference and nonchalance to protect themselves against being hurt. This further frightens the woman, making her think he is going to reject her. So she clings tighter to the relationship and is willing to give in and take even more blame to gain love and acceptance from her partner.

Abuse victims often have a warped sense of familiarity and comfort in an abusive relationship. They will often return to the relationship or, after leaving it, will unconsciously seek out another similar one.

This meeting of two wounded souls, the abused and abuser, creates the perfect set-up for a match made in hell. The abuser attracts someone who is willing to take the abuse and give into his or her control. The victim attracts someone who needs to dominate and control. Both express their pain in opposite but destructively codependent ways.

Neither the victim nor the abuser is helping themselves or the relationship by resorting to the more extreme reactions typical of their genders.

Men would do well to restrain their angry reactions and spend more time internalizing the situation and considering their own part in it. Women could greatly benefit from acknowledging and expressing their anger in healthy ways, standing up for their opinions, and demanding their partners accept responsibility for his or her actions.

But this is easier said than done, as many of the relationship problems between victims and abusers come from unhealthy or inadequate behavioral patterns learned both in childhood and reinforced throughout their lives. These patterns become so ingrained, they are almost automatic.

Victims of emotional abuse tend to feel unable to set boundaries or feel in control of their own lives. Without a history of witnessing or experiencing healthy, loving relationships, and with weakened self-esteem, they lack trust in their judgment and don't have a realistic perspective from which to see with clarity and objectivity what's right and what's wrong.

Says relationship therapist Michael Formica,

> *[The victim] has little sense of his/her own social value, but makes an effort to establish that value by losing him/herself to the demand for submission. The fear that feeds this insecurity is also about not being lovable or loved, and there is a willingness to accept the inconsistency of the abuser's attention for the sake of being loved.*

Strangely enough, the abusers are also insecure and fear not being lovable. They also don't want to appear weak and vulnerable. Of course, there are different types of abusers and different levels of abuse, but all abusers seek to avoid pain and find love in the only way they know how—through control and intimidation.

Abusers are psychologically or emotionally immature, and they too have never been able to learn healthy, positive ways to interact with others.

An abusive relationship involves two people in pain. Both people must play their role for the abuse to develop and the relationship to fall apart.

Because the abuser is the person inflicting the pain, he or she must accept responsibility for the harm done to the victim/partner. But the victim must also take responsibility for implementing change once he or she is aware that the partner's behavior is abusive.

Once victims have more insight about the type of relationship they are involved in or tend to develop, it's important that they accept personal responsibility for creating boundaries and initiating change. They can *learn* how to stand up for themselves within their current relationship, or make the decision to start over and develop relationships with other kinds of people.

When we have the courage to honestly examine our own natures and the nature of our relationships, then we can decide what is acceptable and unacceptable to us. With this choice, we are able to live and love peacefully, authentically, and with mindful awareness.

The point is to learn there are better and healthier ways to relate to others. As you get a better insight about yourself, your abuser, and how abusers function, you'll have more knowledge and power to make decisions about your life moving forward.

# Chapter 7:
# Your Unfinished Business

*"She is still a prisoner of her childhood;*
*attempting to create a new life,*
*she reencounters the trauma."*

—Judith Lewis Herman

As someone living with an emotional abuser, you may have some unfinished business from your own past. I'm not talking about a project you haven't completed or some bills left unpaid.

Unfinished business is a therapy term related to the emotions and memories surrounding past experiences you've avoided or repressed, often related to an early abuser.

When the painful feelings of the past event aren't dealt with at the time, they tend to crop up later in unexpected and damaging ways. You block out or repress these past events because the feelings are too difficult or traumatic to face.

The pain of the past can be overwhelming, so to function, you might choose to minimize or ignore the feelings. This is especially true when you were a child and didn't have the coping skills or maturity to handle emotional abuse or other traumatic events.

Without the ability to resolve the situation or manage the pain, all the early negative emotions are trapped inside you.

Your unfinished business includes all the adult ways you would have been able to respond to your pain had you possessed the skills and strength as a child. This includes the ability to express feelings you haven't expressed, say things to your abuser that need to be said, release the false hopes about your abuser you might still cling to, and resolve conflicts that are still brewing with this person.

When you repress these past wounds and don't tend to unfinished business, the feelings linger in the background of your heart and mind, and leak out in the form of sadness, grief, fear, anger, anxiety, low self-esteem, mistrust, or terror.

If left unaddressed, the feelings associated with these events are carried into your present life and play a huge part in your choice of an intimate partner and how you interact with him or her.

Because of unfinished business with your parents or with another former relationship, you were more vulnerable to an emotional abuser. This isn't because you are weak or have poor judgment. When you have unfinished business, the need to repeat the past over and over is unconscious but compelling.

You are caught in a pattern that is deeply ingrained and painful, but all too familiar. Until you sort out the baggage from the past, you may be destined to keep repeating your choices and behaviors, even if you leave your current abuser.

Sorting out the baggage isn't something you can do by yourself or heal overnight. If you suffered emotional or physical abuse, neglect, constant criticism, or trauma as a child, you most certainly will need the help of a licensed, trained counselor to help you heal this emotional trauma.

The idea of counseling may feel overwhelming, especially when you are trying to cope with the day-to-day difficulties of living with an emotional abuser on top of all your other life responsibilities. You may go through a "good" phase with your partner and begin to think all is well. Why should you dredge up all of the "stuff" from the past?

It's tempting to keep hoping he or she will change or to believe you have some magical power to help him finally see the light. But even during calm times, the two of you are stuck in a pattern, and unless you want history to continue repeating, you need to extricate yourself.

This begins by addressing the pain of the original abuse you suffered and acknowledging that your original abuser was indeed abusing you.

From my own experience as the child of an alcoholic, I repeated many patterns I learned as a child, which were coping mechanisms for me. I was a pleaser, peacemaker, and one to forgive and forget even when it wasn't merited. I felt protective of my alcoholic parent and made excuses for the neglect and pain the disease caused me and our family.

It wasn't until I could acknowledge my feelings of abandonment, fear, shame, and anger that I was able to reclaim my inner power and make choices in relationships and life that are healthy and positive. I learned how to balance my adult compassion for my alcoholic parent with the childhood pain that never should have happened to an innocent.

It took the support of a caring, compassionate therapist to help me get to this point. Therapy is important and honorable work that must be undertaken to facilitate healing and personal empowerment. You will likely find great relief to have someone in your corner with whom you can safely unload all the pain and confusion you've been carrying around for years.

I am not a licensed counselor, and it would be a disservice to you and the profession if I attempted to counsel you on your unfinished business and recovering from the pain of your past.

I strongly encourage you to find a therapist, and I provide resources for finding one at the end of this book. You might want to share some of the things you are learning in this book with your counselor.

However, I can tell you what you might expect from a good counselor who is trained in helping people work through past pain and childhood trauma. Your counselor might:

- Ask you to recount how you were emotionally abused as a child (or abused in another way).

- Ask you to express the feelings you had as a child around the abuser's behavior and yourself at the time.

- Conduct some "inner child" work to help you access some of the memories and feelings you had as a child.

- Encourage you to tap into the anger you felt and still might feel toward your original abuser.

- Invite you to mourn the loss of part of your childhood that was taken by the abuse.

- Encourage you to let go of false hope of getting the kind of parent(s) you dreamed of having.

- Work with you on separating emotionally from your original abuser.

- Show you skills for "parenting" yourself.

- Discuss some of the childhood patterns you had with your abusive parent or former abusive partner and how they are playing out in your current abusive relationship.

- Help you separate the two relationships (with your original abuser and your current partner) so you can make a clear decision about your current relationship.

Even if you don't think you have unfinished business, or you're not clear whether you were involved in an emotionally abusive relationship with a parent or someone else in your past, you are currently in an emotionally abusive situation. There is a reason you were attracted to this person and now accept behavior that is by all measures unacceptable.

A therapist provides a safe environment to explore your past and talk about what you might need to resolve it so you can break the pattern of abuse.

The more you avoid facing the past and figuring out how it has impacted your current relationship, the more deeply repressed the feelings become, until one day they burst out when you least expect it. Managing your emotions through therapy puts you in control of how you process your feelings in a secure and caring environment.

If you simply aren't ready to start therapy right now, you can at least begin thinking about some of the answers you'd give a therapist related to the possible therapy questions I outlined earlier.

- Consider what your unfinished business is.

- Get in touch with the feelings you had as a child related to your original abuser, if you had one.

- Allow yourself to feel angry at your abuser and mentally confront him or her (but don't actually confront them without talking to a therapist).

- Think about the ways you may be holding onto hope of things magically changing with your abuser.

- Try to separate emotionally from your original abuser by acknowledging how he or she can no longer hurt you.

- Think about ways you can become a good parent to yourself to heal the child who was wounded long ago.

- Acknowledge how the patterns of relating to your original abuser are reflected in your current relationship.

The more work you do on healing the past, the better equipped you will be to manage the present. As you grow in awareness about how past abuse has impacted your role as a victim of abuse now, the stronger you'll feel in stopping the abusive patterns in your life.

Even if you grew up in a loving, healthy family, it is still beneficial to explore the dynamics of your parents' relationship and how they parented you to better understand what you do and don't want for your own relationship and family now.

Barrie Davenport

# Chapter 8:
# Reclaiming Your Emotions and Finding Your Anger

*"It is wise to direct your anger towards problems—not people; to focus your energies on answers—not excuses."*

—William Arthur Ward

If you've been in an emotionally abusive relationship, your *emotions* have been badly abused. Your feelings and sanity have been systematically attacked and undermined to the point that you question the validity of your emotions—or your feelings have simply flatlined.

One of my readers describes her emotional world by saying this:

*I feel beat down, exhausted, and confused. I really relate to feeling like I'm either the constant cause for anger and disappointment, or I'm crazy. There is no right response, my words get twisted and turned against me, and I feel painted into a*

*corner [from] which there is no escape. I
have experienced severe depression for so
long, and I feel pretty hopeless that it will
ever end.*

Hopelessness and depression are the results of
repressed emotions. And if you were emotionally
abused as a child, you learned from an early age
how to stuff your emotions so you didn't have to
feel the pain. You simply lost touch with your
emotions.

Another reaction you may experience with
repression is dramatic and unpredictable emotional
eruptions. Your pain suddenly rises to the surface,
and you lash out at anyone in your path. This
makes you feel more out of control and frightened
at your own erratic state of mind.

After years of stuffing your emotions and trying so
hard to keep them contained, it seems like your
psyche is betraying you when you lose it so
unexpectedly.

When this happens, you may try harder to repress
your feelings because they are so overpowering
and scary. You fear your emotions might unleash a
storm of additional chaos in your already chaotic
life and undermine the shred of normalcy you've
worked so hard to maintain.

In reality, the more you shove down your feelings,
the more likely they are to erupt in ways you don't
want them to. When you are able to express your
emotions in a safe and calm way, you'll discover
you feel more in control of yourself and your

abusive situation. Pulling your emotions into the light of day liberates you to reclaim yourself and your power.

## Feeling Numb

Another unfortunate consequence of cutting yourself off from your emotions is that you disassociate from positive feelings as well as from pain. You are numb to all the experiences of life in your efforts to stay at a distance from the pain of your childhood and your current relationship.

Being so cut off from all your feelings also cuts you off from your true self, the real you who has gotten lost under the armor of self-protection. You may feel you don't have an identity, or you don't know who you are.

Even if you're a master at pushing your emotions away, anger and resentment are two emotions that are probably simmering just beneath the surface of your protective shield.

You have anger and resentment toward your abusive partner, and you may well have residual anger at your original abuser. This anger and resentment are part of the unfinished business you need to resolve as part of the healing process.

By holding in your anger and resentment toward your parents or other early abusers, you are still being victimized by them. You are giving them a tremendous amount of your emotional energy that you can't appropriately and safely express.

75

This negative energy is then turned toward yourself, making you feel unworthy, inadequate, and depressed. This is how you get stuck in the past and try to repeat it and change it through your current relationship.

Anger is a natural, healthy emotion when you are able to vent it in a constructive way, rather than through blaming and resentment. When you release your anger in appropriate ways toward your original abuser, you are able to release your grip on the past, empowering you to address the anger you have toward your current abusive partner.

It is as though you are still a child, trying to express your pain and powerlessness through your current abusive relationship. Until you deal with the original abuse as the adult you are now, you won't have the ability to stand up to your current abuser.

So how do you express all this repressed anger in a healthy way? Here are some exercises to help you:

## Write a Letter

One of the best ways to release your anger is by writing a letter to your original abuser and/or current abuser. In this letter, detail everything your abuser did to you that caused you pain, confusion, and anxiety.

Talk about how it made you feel as a child to have no power over the situation and to feel so betrayed and confused.

Let the abuser know how his or her behavior negatively influenced you and damaged your life.

Finally, tell your abuser how you feel about him or her now, and how you intend to live your life moving forward despite the abuse they inflicted on you.

Write this letter in the most empowered, assertive, confident way possible. Try not to write it as a victim, but rather as a healthy-minded, mature adult who is mad as hell and doesn't intend to take it any more.

You may decide to keep the letter, throw it away, or even send it to your original abuser, if it makes you feel better. Don't send the letter to your current abuser at this point until you have gotten stronger and had some discussions with your abuser that we will get to in later chapters.

## Have an Imaginary Conversation

The written word is powerful, but the spoken word is mighty. Pretend your original or current abuser is sitting across from you, put a picture of him or her in a chair, or ask a friend to serve as a stand-in for your abuser.

Then read your letter out loud with all the anger and feeling you've been storing up inside you for years.

If you haven't written a letter, mentally rehearse what you want to say, maybe writing down bullet

77

points to remind you. Then say the words out loud to your abuser.

Allow yourself to get angry—don't hold anything back. This is your opportunity to let them have it for the pain they caused you.

Again, you want to speak the words in an empowered way—not as a victim who is still asking why or begging for love and attention.

# Find a Physical Release

If you've held your anger in for a long time, your body probably needs a huge release of that negative emotional energy. You may have let your feelings out by crying in the past, but crying isn't a powerful enough release for the pent-up rage and pain inside you.

You don't want to show physical aggression toward a person or animal, but you do want to use some dramatic and powerful physical movement to release your feelings.

Some physical releases could include:

- Punching a pillow.
- Kicking a ball into a concrete or block wall over and over.
- Serving a basket of tennis balls over a net with all your strength.
- Doing air-boxing with your imaginary abuser in front of you.

- Boxing with an actual punching bag, viewing it as your abuser.
- Collecting all your aluminum cans and stomping them flat.
- Rolling up a newspaper or magazine and smacking a hard surface with it.

Be creative—you can come up with a variety of safe, nondestructive ways to physically release your anger. Exercise, running, and other physical movement can help release the tension and stress of pent-up anger. Find what feels liberating to you, and practice it whenever you feel anxious, depressed, or overtly angry.

Don't repress your feelings of frustration, helplessness, and anger. Be aware of them, acknowledge them, and take action to expel the buildup of emotional toxins in your body.

## Talk to Your Counselor

One of the safest places to vent your anger is in your counselor's office. He or she can help you identify your anger, which might be misdirected in the form of sadness or anxiety.

Your counselor can invite you to vocalize your deeper feelings of anger in a way that doesn't make you feel overwhelmed or guilty.

You can read your letter to your counselor, or practice your imaginary conversation with someone who is practiced at role playing in these situations.

## Personal Confrontation

At some point, you may want to personally confront your original abuser and let him or her know how they abused or neglected you, how it made you feel as a child, and how it has affected you as a child and an adult. (We'll talk about confronting your current abuser in another chapter.)

If you decide to have this confrontation, you might consider having it in your counselor's office or with another safe person who can support you.

If the abuser was one of your parents, it will be difficult to express your pain and the impact of your childhood abuse, but doing so in a confident, assertive way will take away much of the power this person has held over you.

Just as you did in the imaginary confrontation, you'll want to approach this conversation as an empowered adult who is no longer a helpless victim.

You don't need to yell, ask why, or call the abuser names. You simply want this person to know that his or her behavior was wrong and especially egregious, because you were a child with no one to defend you.

You want the abuser to know how much it hurt you as a child, how much it has impacted your life, and how you intend to no longer accept abuse in your life. You also want him or her to know you are angry. "I am really angry at you for the way you treated me as a child."

It's good to rehearse the confrontation in your head before you meet with the abuser. Decide in advance exactly what you want from this relationship going forward.

If you want to maintain it, you'll need to articulate clearly your expectations. For example, you might say:

- I want you to stop criticizing me and comparing me to my brother.

- I want you to stop defending your bad behavior and accept responsibility for your actions.

- I want you to recognize that I am now an adult and quit trying to manage my life.

- I want us to have a mature, adult relationship where we are kind and loving to each other.

You might want to let your abuser know your fears about moving forward with the relationship. "I'm afraid you'll continue to try to control me." "I'm afraid you'll do something to damage my life again."

Hopefully, he or she will hear you and show some ability to understand your pain and take responsibility. Perhaps this person has grown or received counseling throughout the years and has learned better ways to be in a healthy relationship.

However, it's smart to be prepared for him or her to deny, defend, or deflect. This person might try making you feel guilty, rationalizing his or her behavior, acting like a martyr, or blaming you for what happened.

If he or she does not respond to you positively, you may have to cut off the confrontation and leave the room. But at least you were able to speak your mind and express your anger in an empowered way.

## A New Anger Mindset

Releasing your anger in constructive ways won't change what happened to you and may not change your abuser. But YOU will be changed in a profound way, as you acknowledge the truth of what happened and how you feel about it.

Anger can feel scary and overwhelming, but it doesn't have to. You can start by changing your perspective about anger, by giving yourself permission to feel it.

For most of my adult life, I felt so protective of my alcoholic parent that I didn't allow myself to feel the anger of being neglected as a child. I didn't think I deserved to be angry, because my parent had suffered so much. It wasn't until I accepted and embraced my anger that I was able to regain my strength and confidence in my own relationships.

Women expressing anger are often labeled as bitches, hysterical, or crazy. It's OK if we cry and appear victimized, but showing the strength of anger isn't something culturally endorsed.

In addition to repressing anger because of the pain you've experienced, you have society telling you to pipe down, get a grip, and stay calm.

If you were emotionally abused as a child, you might feel, like I did, that you don't deserve to feel angry or that your situation didn't merit anger. Maybe you even feel guilty about any angry feelings you have.

You might even feel proud that you've been able to cope so well and not lose control or fall apart. But coping hasn't proved to be enough. Now you need to learn a new skill that teaches you anger is acceptable and should be expressed.

By expressing your anger, you will . . .

- Lessen the grip of some of the guilt, shame, and resentment you feel.

- Improve your self-esteem and sense of worthiness.

- Feel as though a burden has been lifted, and you are free of the weight of repressed anger.

- Unlock much of the physical tension that comes with repressed anger.

- Open up to enjoy pleasurable emotions and experiences you couldn't previously enjoy.

- Erase some of the confusion and crazy feelings, as you have more clarity about the truth of your past.

- Be empowered to be emotionally, mentally, and physically stronger.

- Become more independent and adult-like in managing your life and relationships, as you separate emotionally from your parents or original abuser.

- Be given you the clarity to choose better relationships and to enjoy the positive relationships you already have.

- Allow you to forgive yourself and other people more easily.

Perhaps even thinking about your buried anger right now is bringing some of it to the surface for you. Try not to shove the feelings back down, but instead take advantage of them now, and work on the anger exercises outlined previously while your feelings are fresh.

If you find your feelings are too overwhelming, take a break and go for a short walk or call a friend to talk. Also, discussing your anger in therapy is an important part of your healing process, and I encourage you to ask your therapist to help you bring it to the surface safely.

You have every reason and right to feel angry. Use your anger for fuel, and ride the force of your anger to stand up for yourself and your basic, human right to be treated with love and respect.

Barrie Davenport

# Chapter 9:
# Creating Your Personal
# Operating System

*"I am no bird; and no net ensnares me: I am a free human being with an independent will."*

—Charlotte Bronte

When you've been the victim of emotional abuse, you may find you have lost your faith in your judgment and opinions. You may not know what you believe any more, and you've lost your sense of right and wrong, good and bad, love and pain.

Your abusive partner has manipulated and controlled his or her way into the dictator position of your relationship, and, as a result, your identity has been steamrolled right out of you.

You may find you look outside for affirmation and reinforcement, because you don't have a blueprint for how to conduct your life, how to think, and how to feel.

Barrie Davenport

When your self-esteem and confidence are low,
you look to others to approve you, prop you up,
give permission, or sanction your behavior. By
doing this, you give away your authenticity and
personal power.

The abuse makes you feel like a helpless child who
has no control over decisions and consequences.
In fact, you may find you revert to the behaviors of
childhood when your parents defined and approved
your choices and behaviors. You may simply roll
over and allow your abuser to take the wheel
because you feel so powerless.

As an adult, you know this need for outside
approval is no longer necessary. In fact, it is
counterproductive to your personal growth and
happiness, making you dependent on others for
your well-being and security.

Even though we don't want to give away our
personal power, often we simply don't know how to
claim it. We haven't taken the time to define who
we are and what we want from life. Or we're too
afraid to claim it because our abuser might become
angry or upset and create further chaos.

You may not feel you have the choice to define
your own personal operating system. You may feel
so uncomfortable and obligated to live through an
operating system defined by your partner, that it
never occurs to you that you might have your own
opinions, beliefs, and sound judgments.

You've been living on autopilot, simply reacting to
whatever happens to come your way, rather than

proactively defining your life and your relationships on YOUR terms rather than your partner's or your parent's or any other person's.

Deep inside every person is the profound longing to live authentically. Deep inside we want to live the life we define for ourselves, not one defined by the chains of abuse.

We may not consciously understand that longing, but if this need is not met, our pain and longing come out in unhealthy and self-destructive ways—through depression, resentment, anxiety, passive-aggressive behaviors, and physical illness.

We've explored why abuse has stifled you and forced you to accept a way of life that holds you back. We've looked at the emotions you have suppressed and the anger you haven't been able to ventilate properly.

Now let's dig deeper to think about how you can define your own personal operating system for your life, even if you don't think you can implement it right away.

If you don't know what a personal operating system is, let me give you a quick overview. Your personal operating system (or POS) is your worldview, your life orientation—how you consciously define your world and choose to operate within it. It includes your belief systems, values, outlooks, integrity, opinions, likes and dislikes, and personal boundaries.

When you lack personal power, as you do in an abusive relationship, the prevailing operating system is a problem-focused, anxiety-based, and reactive way of being. Living in a hostile and pain-oriented relationship, you have honed the "fight, flight, or freeze" reaction to life experience. You are constantly in a state of responding and reacting, rather than deciding and creating.

When you design your POS, you are empowering yourself for a new and more dynamic life orientation that isn't fear-based. You are developing a set of authentic choices and actions for meeting life experience more effectively, joyfully, and with much greater fulfillment and purpose.

This may feel impossible right now when you are living with someone who wants to control and manipulate you. But you can start creating your system even before you have the strength or will to implement it.

## Defining Your POS

Simply by defining your personal operating system, you'll feel more self-worth and more authentic. You'll recognize that you do have your own opinions, beliefs, and points of view, which may or may not coincide with your partner's.

Your POS is wholly independent of what your partner may expect from you. And by getting fiercely clear about what YOU want for your life, you'll give yourself an infusion of strength and inner resolve to claim it.

Let's talk about how you can create and implement your own personal operating system. This isn't something you can achieve overnight, as it involves both changing the abuse and healing from the pain it has caused you—which we'll discuss later in the book.

It will involve making some actual changes in the way you live your life and how you allow other people to treat you and behave around you. It's a work in progress, but once you have this blueprint, you'll see the way forward much more clearly.

Right now, in this moment, start to think about how you might change everything in your life if you had a chance for a do-over. Not that you will change everything. There are some things working well in your life.

But shift your mental orientation to see that you have the power to recreate and begin again with many of your choices, beliefs, actions, and relationships, even if you feel insecure or frightened right now.

Creating your personal operating system requires you examine every area of your life to determine whether or not it is in accordance with *your own* desires, beliefs, and preferences rather than your abuser's.

You won't be able to change everything, at least not right away, but you can change enough to boost your self-esteem significantly.

To help you get started, answer the following questions about different areas of your life. These questions are designed to help you see what has been taken away or negated in your relationship with an abusive partner, and how you would redefine or recreate these things on your own terms.

# Relationships

- What relationships are working well in your life right now? What do you like and enjoy about them? How are you treated in these relationships?

- What relationships (other than your intimate relationship) drain you of energy, make you feel bad, or simply don't support your authentic self? How could you improve the relationship or release it? What actions are you willing to take?

- What relationship behaviors do you need to change or improve to have healthy, positive interactions with the people you want in your life?

# Career

- What do you find fulfilling and enjoyable about your work right now?

- What aspects of your work do you dislike or feel don't reflect what you really want to be doing in your career?

- What actions can you take right now to begin making positive changes with your work or career?

## Health

- In what ways are you currently taking care of your health and physical well-being?

- What healthy behaviors, choices, or activities would you like to adopt that you aren't practicing right now?

- What actions are you willing to take to create the healthy lifestyle you desire?

## Personal Beliefs

- What personal beliefs about childrearing, money management, important values, religion, politics, friendships, family, or any other area have you not developed for yourself because your spouse or partner (or parents, family, friends, etc.) has enforced his or her beliefs onto you?

- What are your personal beliefs related to these important areas of your life that you don't feel comfortable embracing or expressing right now? (If you aren't sure what they are, spend some time thinking about it, doing research, looking for positive role models, etc., so you can form your own opinions.)

- How are you willing to express and act on some of these important personal beliefs, even if they differ from your spouse or partner's beliefs?

## Learning and Skills

- How are you continuing to learn new skills, gain knowledge or expertise, or expand yourself through learning?

- What other skills, knowledge, or expertise would you like to acquire to become more confident, empowered, and independent?

- What actions are you willing to take now or in the near future to acquire those things?

## Integrity

- What is your philosophy and belief system for living with integrity? How are you currently living with integrity in your life?

- How are you living against your system of integrity or ignoring your integrity?

- What actions are you willing to take right now to restore your integrity?

## Other

- What other areas of your life would you like to include in your personal operating system not mentioned above?

- How would you like to define your personal operating system for these areas?

Of course, the biggest part of your operating system that has been lost is your vision of a happy, healthy, intimate connection with the person you love. You may feel so out of touch with what your ideal relationship is that you don't know where to begin. We'll review what real love means and what a healthy relationship looks like later in the book.

As you get stronger and more self-aware, you'll want your own operating system for your love relationship. You will need to redefine areas where you aren't clear about what your own system is and what is borrowed (or enforced) from your partner or elsewhere.

Question all your political or religious beliefs, the way you raise your children, how you interact with friends and family, what you wear, how you present yourself to others, what kind of work you do, how you handle money, how you spend your free time, the way you make decisions, and how you perceive yourself.

Ask yourself constantly, "Is this really what I think, feel, or believe? Is this really what I want, or is it what my abuser wants from me?"

This exercise will take some time, as you may feel stumped with some of these areas of your life. You may want to read or research to help define a particular position, or look to people you respect and admire to gain clarity on your future choices and behaviors.

You might feel anxiety while taking personal responsibility for choices and decisions your spouse has arbitrarily hijacked, even though you resent his or her stripping you of your identity.

All these are normal feelings, but they shouldn't deter you from creating your POS, even if it takes some time to act on it. Personal responsibility is the key to freedom and empowerment.

With every decision you make for yourself and every act of self-creation, you're moving closer to the real you and building a foundation of strength and confidence that will continue to grow.

Whether you make the decision to stay in your relationship and work on it or to leave the relationship to begin again, you'll be prepared to live life on the terms and within a framework you've designed for yourself.

Barrie Davenport

# Chapter 10:
# Finding Your Power,
# Building Your Boundaries

*"You gain strength, courage and confidence by every experience in which you really stop to look fear in the face. You are able to say to yourself, 'I have lived through this horror. I can take the next thing that comes along.' You must do the thing you think you cannot do."*

—Eleanor Roosevelt

Whether you stay in the relationship for another week, another year, or a lifetime, you can no longer accept emotional abuse from your partner. You simply can't.

You know too much now, and there's no pretending the behavior is normal, acceptable, or deserved. No matter what the reasons behind it, no matter how wounded your partner may have been, no matter how much you love him or her, abuse is wrong, plain and simple.

You need to commit to yourself that you won't tolerate it any longer. Your acceptance of the abuse is over, and you mean it.

Of course, stopping the abuse and changing your responses to it is not a quick or easy proposition. You must be prepared for uncomfortable, even angry, pushback from your partner. You must also be willing to look at your own patterns of behavior and change them, beginning now.

So how do you take a stance against the abuse, stand up to your partner, and let him or her know you've drawn a line in the sand? And how do you know they'll stop the abuse even when you do take a stand?

Let's start with the initial confrontation with your partner to let him or her know your new state of mind. Take a deep breath, because I'm sure the thought of this makes you feel anxious, which is perfectly normal.

An abuser wants to keep you anxious and off balance, because this anxiety keeps you dependent and unsure. It can also trigger your childhood pain and fear.

But there's an important distinction you need to remember. You are now an adult with personal power. You're no longer the helpless child who couldn't stand up to your abuser. And your partner isn't your original abuser, even if it feels the same. Let the adult in you do the talking.

If you were a confident, strong person before you met your abuser, step into the shoes of that former self when you have this initial meeting.

## Stating Your Case

There are two ways to state your case and announce your new position. You can either wait until the next incident of abuse occurs and address the incident, along with your new position about not tolerating it any longer. Or you can set a specific day and time to discuss the abusive patterns with your spouse or partner.

Based on your particular relationship, you'll need to decide whether it's better to talk in the moment of an abusive event or to approach your partner at another time for a discussion. Some abusers are unaware (or in denial) of their abusive behaviors, so it can be useful to call them out on it in the moment—but not if they are going to blow up and storm away.

Whether you decide to wait until an abusive event occurs to take your stand or initiate a conversation, prepare yourself mentally and emotionally before that day or hour arrives. Think about what you want to say, how you are going to say it, and what you'll do based on your abuser's response.

For example, let's say your abuser makes a rude or sarcastic comment to you. As soon as it happens, look your partner in the eye (or ask him or her to look at you), and frame your response calmly but firmly, using "I feel" statements rather than accusatory statements.

You might say, "I feel disrespected and unloved when you say that to me. It feels like a put down, so please don't say it again."

At this point, your partner might be defensive or try to blow you off, and this is when you say, "There's something more I need to tell you."

If you are initiating a conversation without waiting for an abusive event, tell your partner you have something you need to discuss, and go into a quiet room without distraction or children nearby.

Begin the conversation by saying you have been unhappy about the way your relationship is going. You need to implement some changes and hope your partner is also interested in improving the relationship.

You might mention that you have been doing some reading about healthy relationships, and that you have learned some of his or her behaviors make you feel emotionally abused. Then offer some specific examples related to ONE area of the abuse for now. Don't overwhelm your partner with a litany of complaints. Start with the offense that hurts or bothers you most.

You might say, "Last week when you criticized me in front of your parents, I felt embarrassed and shamed. It felt like you didn't love me or care about my feelings. Maybe you aren't aware of your critical remarks and how they hurt me, but they are rude and I would appreciate it if you would stop making them altogether."

If you can continue without your partner getting angry, discuss your childhood abuse and how your partner's behavior triggers the pain you had as a child and makes you react even more strongly. You might say something like, "When you criticize me, it reminds me of how my mom would put me down and try to make me feel stupid."

Try hard to avoid labeling, blaming, or shaming your partner in this conversation, and try not to use the words "always" and "never" when describing or referring to your partner's behavior. Taking this stance may be surprising or new to your abusive partner, so again, be firm but kind.

If your partner responds openly or at least without anger or defensiveness, show him the list of abusive behaviors listed at the end of this book. Try to explain more about emotional abuse and why both of you are trapped in this pattern. Let him or her know your goal and desire is to build a mutually loving, respectful, and intimate relationship.

One last statement you might want to include in this conversation is this: "I have been feeling unhappy about this for a long time, and I know I haven't said much about it or let you know how I feel. But now I am, and I want you to know I will no longer accept it."

It is unlikely that abusers can change cold turkey without therapy. First, they need to be highly motivated to change, and also they need support in learning how to change. When you state that you will no longer accept the behavior, you must let your abuser know you want them to begin therapy as part of your new mindset.

## Your Partner's Reaction

How your partner reacts to this conversation will give you important information about where you'll go from here. If he or she is immediately defensive, angry, and shifts the blame to you, it's a good indicator that the relationship is in serious trouble.

If your partner refuses therapy and says he or she can change on their own, you know they aren't committed to improving your relationship.

However, if your partner listens and shows some willingness to address the problem, you have something to work with.

Either way, continue to be consistent in your responses to abusive behavior or words. The *moment* they occur, point them out and let your partner know you don't like the behavior. Again, be calm but firm. "I do not like the way you are speaking to me, and I will not tolerate it."

If the abuse continues or escalates, walk away with the statement, "I'm not going to stand here and take this. We can talk when you're ready to be calm and speak respectfully."

Have a plan in mind for what you will say and do when the abuse occurs in various situations. It may be hard to take your stand and walk away if you are with other people, or if you're out at a restaurant with just the two of you. But this is a powerful message to your abusive partner, especially if you have the courage to stand up for yourself when others are present.

## Plan in Advance

Decide now what you'll do in these situations to let him or her know you mean business. You may need to politely excuse yourself, call a cab, and go home. You may get up from the table and leave the restaurant for a few minutes. Or you may simply decide to point out the abuse, state that you don't like it, and continue on. Whatever you do, don't simply allow it to occur unchecked.

If your abusive spouse or partner is angry with you, acknowledge the anger by saying, "I see you are angry with me, but we can't talk unless we are calm." By acknowledging the anger, you may diffuse it to certain extent.

If the anger continues, this is the time to calmly announce you need to walk away or leave the space altogether. Be sure you leave the door open for future communication by saying, "I can't stay if you are going to continue talking this way, but I'll be ready to talk when you are calmer (or kinder, or less critical)."

Do your best not to get into a verbal battle with your partner or allow him or her to draw you into an argument. This gives your abuser ammunition to shift the blame to you.

This change of events will be hard for both of you. Your partner certainly didn't see this coming and may become more abusive before deciding you mean business. You may find yourself falling back into old patterns and feel more anxious than you did prior to taking your stance.

But if your partner sees you back down or behave inconsistently, he or she will gain even more power over you, and you'll feel worse about yourself.

Hopefully your partner will respond positively to your boundaries and see that you want to heal the relationship (if indeed you do). If you get a more positive reaction, this is the time to again suggest counseling for both of you.

You may have both been wounded as children and entered the relationship with your own fears, insecurities, intimacy issues, and lack of trust. You will both need to take responsibility for your roles and behaviors in the dynamic between you, even if your reactions haven't been abusive. Your couple's counselor may suggest individual therapy for one or both of you.

As you continue to work on your unfinished business from your childhood and show more assertiveness with your partner, you'll feel more and more in control of your life and more empowered to make decisions about your relationship.

Even if your partner remains abusive, you'll diminish the impact the abuse has on you by standing firm with your boundaries.

Barrie Davenport

# Chapter 11:
# Empowerment through Action

*"Remember, a real decision is measured by the fact that you've taken new action. If there's no action, you haven't truly decided."*

—Tony Robbins

In the last chapter, we talked about finally confronting your abuser, taking a stance for what you will no longer accept, and setting boundaries for dealing with continued abuse as long as you are with your abuser.

I'm sure you know that making change in yourself and seeing change in your abuser, if that happens, will not happen quickly.

Your priority is making an ongoing *investment in yourself*, first and foremost. You can do this by learning what normal, healthy behavior is and practicing it until it becomes ingrained in your mind and your actions.

Knowing exactly what you will and won't accept from your partner and learning more about the qualities of healthy, loving relationships helps you have principles in place. These principles must take precedence over your attempts to change or understand your abusive partner.

Consistent action by calling out your partner on abuse and demanding your rights and boundaries is necessary to break the patterns of abuse—even if your partner doesn't change. For your own mental health, you need to feel powerful and self-assured that you won't roll over and take it any longer.

## Power Questions for Change

Part of feeling empowered is being prepared. Abusive behaviors and words can come out of left field and throw you for a loop. In the heat of the moment, you may be too shocked, numbed, or wounded to come up with a confident reply.

Having a plan of action helps you know what to say and do when your abuser strikes.

Here are some questions to ask yourself to help you build your plan of action for managing your partner and your own reactions:

- What is your go-to statement when the abuse occurs the next time? (For example, you might say, "Stop. This is exactly the abusive behavior I've been talking about.")

- What exactly do you plan to say to your partner to call him out on his behavior or words? (For example, you might say, "I find this hurtful and demeaning. It is unacceptable for someone who is supposed to love me to say something like that.")

- What do you know about yourself and your reactions to your partner that might be contributing to the problem?

- What changes do you intend to make to be emotionally healthy and less victimized?

- How can you practice assertiveness in your language and your reactions with your emotional abuser?

- What are some specific things you want to speak your mind about? What will you say?

- What beliefs and fears have held you back from speaking your mind?

- How are you being overly polite and accommodating or pushing down your own desires because you don't want to upset your partner?

- Do you have the strength right now to let go of your fears?

- What confident actions will you now take to show your abuser he can no longer control you?

- Where will you begin to reclaim your power? What activities and interests can you pursue that will boost your confidence and joy?

## Excusing Your Abuser

To end the abuse and for your own empowerment, it's critical that you are honest about how you have been trying to change, cajole, win over, or tiptoe around your abuser to "help" him or her see the light. How much personal responsibility have you taken for "curing" your partner of his or her abusive ways?

It's true your partner has emotional issues and wounds, and these may be the source of his or her behavior. But you cannot erase your partner's past nor change the current behavior. Change is totally up to your partner's discretion. You only have power over yourself and your choices and actions.

One of the big mistakes that abuse victims make is focusing a lot of time and energy trying to understand their abuser, why they behave the way they do, and what the victim can do to improve their abuser's behavior.

It's useful to know the mind and motivations of your abuser insofar as it helps YOU to see what you're dealing with and allows you enough understanding and compassion to deal with the issues constructively.

However, as you've learned, emotional abusers are excellent at manipulation and will have you questioning yourself before you know it. When they continue to make excuses, lie to you repeatedly, or try to make you feel guilty for confronting them, you must address their behaviors, rather than excusing them as insecure, "in denial," or wounded themselves.

You must recognize that despite their internal issues or past pain, they are adults who are determined to place themselves above the generally accepted rules for behavior—or to defy them outright.

Ask yourself how your abuser's behavior compares to your principles for respectful and loving behavior. This should be your *only* measuring stick for how you respond and act.

If you let them off the hook or respond to their guilt trips, you lose your one and only power—the power of choice. You have the power to choose your actions, and only action will get the attention of your abuser. Not empty threats, not understanding, and not accepting guilt or blame.

The action you take doesn't always have to be drastic, but it must be firm, decisive, and in *your* interest. Through consistent action, your abuser will get the message that you're not about to be abused, exploited, or manipulated any more. *But remember, never, ever threaten action you don't intend to follow through on.*

For example, in the heat of the moment, if you yell at your spouse, "If you criticize me one more time, I'm leaving you," then you better be prepared to leave. If you say, "I find that remark unacceptable," you better not accept it the next time it's spoken, as it most likely will be spoken again. Otherwise, you'll lose all credibility with your partner, and the abusive behaviors will escalate.

## Creating an If/Then Plan

You may have great intentions for change, but in the heat of the moment when your abuser is bullying or manipulating you, you may get tongue-tied or intimidated and not know what to say.

Advance preparation is the key to having a powerful, calm response for most of the abusive scenarios you've come to expect from your partner. That's why it's important to create an if/then plan so you'll know exactly what to say in these situations.

List all the abusive behaviors that your partner exhibits that undermine your relationship principles and that you identify as abusive. For each of these behaviors, write out your if/then plan.

Here are some examples:

- If my partner calls me names, then I will let him know his words are hurtful and mean, and I won't tolerate them. If he responds defensively, then I will leave the room.

- If my partner criticizes the meal I prepare, then I will tell her I won't be preparing meals for the next few days. She is on her own.

- If my partner starts yelling and screaming, then I will take the kids and go to my sister's house for the weekend.

- If my partner tries to blame me for our conflict, I will refuse the blame and redirect our conversation to her actions.

What is your if/then plan when your partner does the following?

If my partner criticizes me, then I will . . .

If my partner blames me, then I will . . .

If my partner yells or gets angry, then I will . . .

If my partner sulks, then I will . . .

If my partner tries to guilt-trip me, then I will . . .

If my partner tries to control me, then I will . . .

If my partner tries to manipulate me, then I will . . .

If my partner gets defensive or sarcastic, then I will . . .

If my partner ignores me, then I will . . .

If my partner embarrasses me in front of others, then I will . . .

If my partner tries to confuse me or act like I'm crazy, then I will . . .

Write down your responses to these if/then situations, and keep them handy to review daily, if necessary. You want to mentally rehearse them enough that you can recall what you want to say when your abuser gets started with his or her bad behaviors.

## Staying on Track

In conversation or requests for behavior change with your partner, if you don't get a simple, direct response, don't succumb to any diversionary tactics.

Ask again or restate your intentions and actions. Stay focused and on message. Make it clear that you're steadfast in pursuit of your relationship principles and the actions you intend to take.

That's the way to maintain self-assertion in an atmosphere where your partner is trying to frighten you, manipulate you, or diminish your power to stand up for yourself.

In many ways, dealing with your emotional abuser is like dealing with a difficult teenager who only responds to consequences rather than words or heart-to-heart talks.

You may feel selfish and unloving by standing up for yourself, but you are initiating a tough-love approach that focuses directly on your core relationship principles and the actions you'll take if they are crossed by your partner.

Teenagers are known for following you around, trying to reengage you in the argument, and guilt you into changing your mind. Manipulators use many of the same tactics.

As you know, many victims of emotional abuse are hesitant to deal with the abusive behavior and their abuser directly. They walk on eggshells, carefully weighing everything they say and do, and taking on way too much responsibility for approaching issues in a way that doesn't offend, upset, or irritate the abuser.

Victims have a false belief that by approaching issues indirectly and not asking for what they really want, they are more likely to "win over" the abuser and save themselves from the pain and discord that's always lurking.

Unless you fear physical abuse, stand tall in front of your abuser, and don't allow him or her to bully you into silence or tears.

A primary tool for your personal empowerment is making your needs and wants known in a clear, simple, straightforward manner and asking questions in a way that leaves little room for ambiguity. "I want you to stop cursing at me right now. It is disrespectful and mean, and I won't stand for it."

Once you have spoken up clearly for yourself, what should you expect from your abuser? The goal again is simple, direct, straightforward, and unambiguous responses and answers to your questions or requests. Anything short of that is an attempt to manipulate or confuse you.

Says Dr. George Simon, author of the book, *In Sheep's Clothing,*

> *For a person really to empower themselves in their lives and relationships, you must be aware of how these tools all fit and work together. A person who respects boundaries, sets limits, won't excuse inappropriate conduct, keeps communication direct, etc. makes his or her needs known and makes decisions about how to respond to actions and situations that threaten those needs. All this can be done without hostility, blaming, resentment, or undue fanfare. It's simply a matter of taking care of oneself and not feeling responsible for anything or anyone else.*

By following these behavioral changes, you will invest your time, attention, and emotional energy where you have power—within yourself.

Your consistent, firm actions will speak volumes about what you will and won't accept in your life. Don't let fear, intimidation, and anxiety hold you back. The more you exercise your power muscle, the stronger it becomes.

One of my readers shared the profound aha moment when she finally realized her power. She says . . .

*After praying for strength and guidance . . . I woke up! I realized I'm 10 times stronger than this moron! I announced, "You no longer have power over me! I'm taking my life back and you are NOT going to be in it!"*

*I ignore his relentless texts, phone calls, and threats. He no longer exists in my mind, and I'm feeling stronger every day! It's a shame to allow another human to steal years from your life. I'm now stronger and more aware of the signs. I've learned that NO OTHER PERSON will ever complete you. Inner peace and true happiness can only be found within.*

Whether or not your awakening leads to the end of your relationship, you do need to wake up and take action. Have a plan. Implement it consistently, and teach your abuser that a new day has dawned in your relationship.

You are strong enough to stand up for yourself and reject the abusive behavior you've lived with for so long.

Barrie Davenport

# Chapter 12:
# Protecting Your
# Children against Abuse

*"Your first obligation as a parent
is to not bring chaos into your kids' lives."*

—Dr. Laura Schlessinger

If you have children, you have another compelling reason to take a stand against the abuse in your home. You need to protect your children and prevent them from being crushed under the cycle of emotional abuse you and your partner are now engaged in.

Hopefully, neither you or your partner are emotionally or physically abusing your children. Unfortunately, it is quite common for those who have suffered emotional abuse as children or in adult relationships to repeat the pattern by abusing their own children.

It is a common progression for victims of emotional abuse to take out their anger and powerlessness on someone less powerful than themselves.

You may find yourself saying the same cruel things to your child that your mom or dad said to you. You may criticize your child for the same things your spouse criticizes you.

This abuse may happen unconsciously at first, but now is the time to be honest with yourself to see how you might be perpetuating the cycle of abuse.

Because you feel powerless against your original abuser or against your current partner, you look for a convenient way to vent your feelings and pain. You must understand that your children aren't equipped to deal with your wounds and the abusive behaviors you may be passing down to them.

For this reason alone, it is imperative you work on your unfinished business with your original abuser and any past abusive relationships. It's all too common to project our own feelings of low self-esteem, guilt, fear, anger, and shame onto our children.

Children can unknowingly trigger abusive behaviors in their victim-parent by reminding the parent of their abusers or by exhibiting some behavior that brings up painful memories.

If you catch yourself using abusive behavior or words with your child, apologize right away, and explain to your child that you will try hard never to do it again.

Children are quick to forgive, but you must take full responsibility and correct the behavior—and remain vigilant that you don't repeat it. Your children are innocent and helpless in the face of abuse, and you must do everything in your power not to take out your pain on them.

Here are some ways to avoid emotionally abusing your kids:

- First, try to accept and love your children for exactly who they are. Let go of unrealistic or demanding expectations, and allow your kids to make mistakes and learn from natural consequences.

- Don't expect your children to fulfill needs a child shouldn't be expected to fulfill. They can't be your confidant, therapist, or best friend. They can't take care of you. You must take care of them.

- Treat your children with loving respect. Your job as a parent is to raise them to be good citizens and to become independent. You aren't their dictator. Offer them the basic dignity and respect that all humans deserve.

- Show them you are a strong, empowered parent by standing up for yourself and refusing to accept poor treatment from your spouse. You are a role model for them to see what self-respect looks like.

- You may feel guilty or sad about any emotionally abusive treatment your child has endured, but don't allow guilt to prevent you from setting appropriate boundaries and discipline with your child. Children need clear limits and consequences so they grow to respect authority and respect the boundaries of others.

- Keep working on yourself and your knowledge of what it takes to be an effective, loving parent. Parenting can be challenging even in the healthiest households. You have more stresses and challenges due to the emotional abuse, and therefore you need more support and information to make sure you are the parent you need to be.

Your partner may also exhibit his abusive behaviors with your children for the same reasons he or she abuses you. If he constantly criticizes, berates, belittles, teases, or frightens your child, this is abuse and must be stopped, and you must be the one to stop it. There is no one else in the home who can protect your children from the lifelong pain of emotional abuse.

Once you take a stand for what you will no longer accept, you also need to take a stand for your children. There is a big difference between loving and appropriate discipline and severe and unjust punishment, manipulation, and control. If you are anxious and fearful around your abuser, you can only imagine how your children must feel.

Says one of my readers,

> *Once I saw it affecting my daughters, I had to go. I refused to allow my kids to think this is how a man is supposed to treat you. I*

*saved and played nice as best as I could. After moving in with other family members twice, going to the city shelter three times. I look back sometimes and say "What took me so long?"*

As I mentioned earlier, taking a stand may escalate the abuse temporarily for everyone in the household, including your children. If your partner attempts to control his abuse around you, he may find another outlet for his bad behavior in your children.

If you see this happening, you need to intercede immediately and protect your children from further abusive treatment. This may feel scary for you, as your partner will likely see this as you undermining his or her authority. Your love and concern for your children's well-being must trump every other consideration.

Before any further abuse of your children can occur, insist that your spouse enter counseling to address his abusive behaviors. You and the children should also enter counseling so they can have a safe way to vent their fear, anger, and pain.

If your spouse refuses to cooperate, then you may need to take more drastic measures. Document any emotionally abusive behaviors your partner exhibits toward your children, and, if possible, use your phone to record the event, either audio or video. If someone you know witnesses an incident, ask them to write it down and date it.

Keep this evidence hidden until you decide you need to use it. There aren't many laws protecting you or your children from emotional abuse, but a judge will certainly take any evidence into account during divorce and custody proceedings.

You may need to give an ultimatum to your partner by saying that you and the children will move out temporarily until he goes to counseling and works on his abusive behaviors. A separation may be what it takes to open his eyes to his bad behaviors and how they are impacting the family. Perhaps then he will be more open to self-examination and counseling.

Be sure you have a support system in place, the name of a good counselor, and a place to stay lined up before you walk out the door. You will also need to explain to your children why you are leaving the house and what you hope will happen as a result. "Dad needs some time to talk with a doctor about his angry feelings so he doesn't take them out on us. He loves you, but we need to give him time to work on this so he can be the best dad possible."

If your partner refuses counseling or to work on his or her issues, you can't keep your children separated from their parent indefinitely without a court order. Emotional abuse is difficult to prove, and if the abuser is inclined, he or she can try to turn the tables against you.

If you decide to stay in the relationship to protect your children, you will need run interference often and serve as a counterbalance to your spouse's behavior.

If you and your partner divorce or end your relationship, it's highly likely the emotionally abusive partner will get part-time custody of your children, unless physical abuse can be proved or unless you can prove threats of violence, neglect, or evidence of broken objects in your home.

You may not be able to protect your child from emotional abuse 100 percent of the time, but you can educate your child on bullying, controlling and manipulative behaviors, and how to treat people with love and kindness. At some point, they will be able to make their own decision about how they want to be treated and where they want to live.

By offering your children constant support, love, affection, and positive words, you can help neutralize the negative impact of any abuse they have encountered. You can give them a safe place to express their feelings and frustrations without belittling their other parent.

You can model for them appropriate relationship skills and how to exhibit self-respect and confidence. Regardless of how anxious and afraid you might feel around your abusive partner, your children's safety and well-being should be the impetus for action. Don't allow the cycle of emotional abuse to continue.

Barrie Davenport

# Chapter 13:
# Should I Stay or
# Should I Leave?

*"Some of us think holding on makes us strong;
but sometimes it is letting go."*

—Hermann Hesse

This is the big question, and it's probably gone through your head a thousand and one times, along with many other questions.

Can my partner change?

Can our relationship get better?

How will I know when it's time to leave?

Can I make it on my own?

What will happen to our kids?

What will people think?

Fear and confusion may cloud your ability to take action one way or another. You may really love your partner and see many good qualities in him or her, the qualities that first attracted you. You may feel sympathy, guilt about leaving, or worry that you are breaking a religious or cultural vow.

Whether you stay in the relationship and try to make it better, or you decide to leave and start over, you will face fear and doubt, positives and negatives, along with joy and pain. But if you make your decision with full awareness of the potential outcomes and consequences, you'll feel better about the decision you make, whatever it happens to be.

## Reasons You Must Leave

It's smart to understand reasons you *absolutely should leave,* feeling certain you have made the right choice. There are some reasons that are too compelling to justify remaining with your abuser. Here are eight strong reasons to end your relationship with your abuser:

**1. If your partner is threatening to physically abuse you,** or has already been physically violent toward you, it's time to leave. Physical abusers often begin by emotionally abusing their victims, and if the victim continues to accept the emotional abuse, the behavior will escalate. If he has hit, pushed, or slapped you just once, don't assume it's an isolated incident, even if he was drinking too much. It he was violent once, he will be violent again if you stick around.

**2. If your partner's emotional abuse has pushed you to the point that you have become physically violent** or you're thinking about doing something violent to your partner, you need to leave. Your partner may have pushed you to a breaking point, but abuse is abuse, and both of you could get seriously hurt. If your emotional abuser is a woman, and you are a man, you are putting yourself in danger of arrest or losing your children if you retaliate with physical violence.

**3. If your partner is emotionally or physically abusing your children,** it is your job to protect them above all else. Don't fool yourself that your kids are not being psychologically damaged by abuse. They are. Your spouse is an adult. Your children are not, and they need a responsible, loving parent to remove them from an abusive situation.

**4. If you are emotionally abusing your children** as a result of being the victim of your partner's abuse, you need to be honest with yourself, get out of the relationship, and seek counseling to ensure you don't damage your children. Review the list of behaviors of emotional abuse at the end of this book, and ask yourself if you are exhibiting any of these behaviors with your children. As we've discussed, abuse is a pattern that gets passed around like a contagious disease.

**5. If your children regularly witness you being abused, you must take action.** Even witnessing your spouse emotionally abusing you is abusive for your children. They see you upset, crying, angry, resentful, and diminished. They know intuitively something is wrong, even if you try to hide it. You need to be a good role model for your children by showing them strength and self-respect. Seeing one parent abusing the other with words, actions, or violence is deeply upsetting and confusing for children.

**6. If your partner has a serious mental health disorder or a drug or alcohol abuse problem,** the road to healing and recovery will be much longer with no guaranteed outcome. Your partner will need to be highly motivated to change, and even then you'll face many setbacks as the compulsions for certain behaviors are so strong. This could well be a deal breaker if your partner doesn't have the motivation and discipline to make the necessary changes.

**7. If your mental health is suffering to the point you're incapacitated** or questioning your own sanity, you need to get out of the environment right away and seek treatment with a medical professional. The longer you stay in the abusive relationship, the more likely it is your mental health will suffer, making it impossible to properly care for your family, work, and other responsibilities.

**8. If it's clear your partner takes no responsibility for his or her behavior** and has no interest in counseling or change, and you are suffering and deeply unhappy in the relationship, then it's time to move on. You need to reclaim your life, your energy, and your emotions, and you can't do that with an unwilling, uncooperative partner.

If you recognize one or more of these scenarios as part of your abuse dynamic, it's time to make a firm decision to part ways with your abuser. You can't allow these devastating behaviors to continue if you want to salvage your own mental health and that of any children in your family.

# Reasons to Keep Trying

Now that you know these sound reasons to leave the relationship, you might wonder what good reasons there are to stay. You don't want to continue to live in an abusive relationship, so the obvious question is, can my abuser really change?

According to Lundy Bancroft, author of the book *Why Does He Do That? Inside the Minds of Angry and Controlling Men*, there are some specific changes an abuser needs to make to begin recovery.

They need to . . .

- Admit fully to what they have done.

- Stop making excuses and blaming you or others.

- Make amends to you and your children.

- Accept full responsibility and acknowledge that abuse is a choice.

- Identify their controlling behavior patterns.

- Identify the attitudes that drive their abuse.

- Accept that overcoming their abusive behavior/attitudes can take decades and not proclaim they are "cured" after a counseling session or two.

- Not demand credit or praise for improvements they've made.

- Not treat improvements as excuses for occasional acts of abuse and backsliding.

- Develop respectful, kind, and supportive behaviors with you and your children.

- Carry their weight as a partner, parent, and home manager and share power with you.

- Change how they respond to your pain, anger, and frustrations.

- Change how they behave during conflict or arguments.

- Accept any consequences of their abusive actions without feeling sorry for themselves about the consequences or blaming you or your children for them.

If your spouse has shown a real interest in changing and is willing to go to counseling and work on his or her issues, there is hope for your relationship.

Part of the role of the counselor is to show both of you how you are repeating behaviors from your past and why you have developed this pattern in your own relationship.

Healing the abuse in your relationship will take time—many months, if not years. Both of you will need to learn new ways of relating and interacting with each other, and you both will need to heal from the pain of the past as well as the pain caused in your relationship. You both must decide if you're willing to invest this time and energy to save the relationship.

A partner who has a drug or alcohol problem needs to go a step further and acknowledge the addiction and seek ongoing treatment for it, in addition to working on the abusive behaviors and attitudes.

For you to move beyond the emotional abuse and build a healthy relationship, you and your partner must share three critical connection points: intimacy, sharing, and trust.

Intimacy includes both emotional and sexual intimacy. Sharing means you are equals in the relationship without one of you feeling more entitled or powerful. Trust requires you have each other's backs, and you feel completely safe together. These components must be present for a relationship to work.

# The Wrong Reasons to Stay

One primary reason both men and women decide to remain in an abusive relationship is fear. However, fear is generally not a good reason for staying (unless you fear for your life or physical safety). Fear-based decisions will further disempower you and give more power to your abuser.

You might feel afraid and insecure thinking about being alone, because you're not sure you can make it on your own. This is an especially profound fear for women who are homemakers and take care of the children and whose abusive husbands are the wage earner for the family. These women don't think they have the skills or confidence to make a living and care for the children.

Men can also share this fear, worrying that splitting up will create more financial stress or that they might lose access to their children.

A victim may have lost so much self-esteem, they stay in the abusive relationship because they fear no one else will want them. Perhaps the abuser has even stated as much. If someone is telling you over and over in words and actions that you are unlovable, you begin to believe it.

Whatever your fears happen to be, don't allow fear to be the roadblock preventing you from taking action. Your fears may feel real, but more often than not, they aren't totally based in reality. Tackle fear with facts.

## Tackle Fear with Facts

Speak with an attorney or divorce coach about the divorce laws in your state regarding division of assets, child support requirements, alimony, and any other concerns you might have. Meet with a licensed therapist to discuss your fears and to help you formulate a plan for dealing with them. We'll talk more about dealing with the real issues related to ending an abusive relationship later in the book.

For now, recognize that you need to challenge your fears to make a sound decision about whether or not to leave your relationship. Don't allow fear to paralyze you and keep you stuck, when you know it's not in your best interest to remain in the relationship.

You may also remain in the relationship because you still feel love for your abuser and believe he or she loves you. If you've been together for several years, there is an emotional attachment and bond you have together, despite the abuse.

But don't confuse this bond with healthy, real love. Love and abuse cannot operate together. Abusers cannot offer real love to someone they are controlling, manipulating, and wounding. Victims are likely confusing love with dependence and the hope that their partners will change.

However, when someone is constantly hurting you, any real love you have will erode over time. As you learn more about healthy love and intimacy, you'll see how broken the dependent, fear-based love is in your abusive relationship. It will no longer be acceptable to you.

Guilt and self-blame also keep victims trapped in an abusive relationship. You might believe you haven't done enough to win your partner's affection and respect, or you may feel you deserve the treatment and can't wound your partner more by leaving him or her.

You may try over and over to do things better, but you've probably noticed that no matter how hard you try, it's never enough, and you never get the treatment and love you deserve.

You may feel guilt about breaking marriage vows, hurting your children, letting down your friends and family, or dishonoring your faith if you leave the relationship. It is doubly hard to make this difficult decision when you feel pressured by outside forces to stay in the abusive relationship.

As much pressure as you may feel, guilt about the perceptions or reactions of others is never a reason to stay in an abusive situation. No one else is in your shoes or feels the pain you experience on a daily basis. This is your life, and only you can decide what is best for you.

If you see yourself in any of these unhealthy reasons for staying with your abusive partner, I hope you'll reexamine your beliefs and motives, and come to accept the truth of your situation. As painful and scary as it is to face the truth, the alternative is a lifetime of unhappiness, pain, and mental health issues.

However, should you decide to stay in the relationship for practical or financial reasons, because you're waiting to gain the strength to leave, or because your partner has indicated he or she is willing to go to counseling, then you need to implement the strategies outlined in Chapters 10 and 11 to stop the abuse right now so you can regain your power and self-respect.

Barrie Davenport

# Chapter 14:
# Making the
# Decision to Leave

*"When two people decide to get a divorce, it isn't a sign that they 'don't understand' one another, but a sign that they have, at last, begun to."*

—Helen Rowland

The time will come when you have enough information to help you make the decision to leave the marriage or relationship. Even in the most difficult situations, this is never an easy decision.

Letting go of your hopes and dreams about the relationship and acknowledging it is really over is painful and scary. You will have a host of mixed emotions, self-doubts, second guessing, and fears.

Review the eight reasons you absolutely should leave the relationship outlined in Chapter 13. If your situation falls into any of these situations, the decision should be clear. Even so, you may be paralyzed with fear, unable to envision the possibility of a better life. Cutting the cord can feel like letting go of a lifeline, even when you know it's the best decision.

Sometimes it's good to determine a bottom line for yourself to make such an emotionally charged decision. You need something to help you see beyond your fears and what-ifs to the reality of your future, should you stay with this person.

After all the evidence is in, after counseling (or attempts at counseling), after working on yourself, taking a stand with your partner, and keeping your children's well-being in mind, ask yourself these questions:

- Do you really believe your partner will ever change?

- Has your partner addressed his or her childhood "stuff" that instigated his or her abusive behaviors?

- Has your partner completely stopped abusing you (and/or your children) and makes no excuses or denials?

- Is he or she making a wholehearted effort to build an intimate, equal, and trusting relationship with you?

- Can you envision a happy life with your partner moving forward?

- Do YOU feel the wholehearted desire to work it out with your partner?

If the answer is no to any of these questions, and you've given it some time (six months to a year unless violence is involved, then right away), then you need to decide if you're willing to be unhappy in your relationship for the rest of your life.

You may believe you can't leave because you can't afford to or because you don't want to take your children away from their parent. But your mental health and your children's well-being are far more important.

Even if your partner has worked to drop the abusive behavior and gain more emotional maturity and self-awareness, sometimes there's too much water under the bridge. The pain is too deep, the intimacy has evaporated, and the relationship has simply flatlined.

You may have lost respect for your partner, or you may simply realize your individual histories make it too difficult to rebuild a solid relationship. If there is no foundation of love, respect, and intimacy, you won't be able to sustain the connection over the long haul.

## Getting Support

As you make the decision to end the relationship, you need the support of a counselor as you go through the steps of telling your spouse, talking to your children, navigating the legal system, dividing assets, creating a child custody plan, and managing new boundaries with your former partner.

You will also need the support of your family, friends, religious institution, support groups, and any other people, resources, or organizations you would find helpful.

Although you may feel embarrassed or ashamed that your relationship is ending and that you've lived with an abuser, the people who love you want you to be safe and happy. They want to be there for you, and you need to let them in.

If you're not ready to talk to friends and family about the details behind ending your relationship, you can simply say there were serious problems in the relationship that couldn't be worked out. Tell them that you are feeling particularly vulnerable right now, and that you don't wish to discuss the details, but you do need their support in specific ways.

Then tell them exactly what you need. It could be watching your children, going with you to the attorney's office, or simply going out to lunch with you. Please don't isolate yourself during this really difficult time of your life.

You may be in the situation where you are fully aware you need to leave, but you just aren't strong enough yet to take action. Your self-esteem and assertiveness may not be developed enough to give you the motivation to move forward.

If this is the case, please don't beat yourself up over it. You can use this time to work on yourself, build your confidence and sense of self with a counselor, and get prepared for the time you do take action. Preparation for this step is essential, and there are many plans you can make before you implement them.

## The Bright Side

I know the entire process of ending your relationship feels daunting, and we'll talk about some of the specific ways you can prepare yourself and your children in the next chapters. But for now, I'd like to remind you of all the positive outcomes you will experience once you've made this decision.

- You will no longer be subjected to emotional abuse on a daily basis.

- You'll have more time and energy to focus on you and what's important to you.

- You will have a peaceful, calm household for you and your children.

- You will no longer feel like you're walking on eggshells every day.

- You'll be able to focus on healing yourself, improving your self-esteem, and developing new patterns of behavior.

- You'll find your anxiety and depression abates.

- You'll have the freedom to make your own choices and decisions.

- You'll be able to spend more time with people you care about without worry.

- You'll learn more about healthy relationships and what to look for in a love partner.

- You'll have the freedom to develop a new, loving relationship with a healthy minded person.

As you make the decision to end the relationship, keep your attention focused fully on your needs and the needs of your children. Your partner may sense a shift in you or your attitude and may suspect something is about to change.

He or she may escalate guilt trips, blame and shame tactics, and bullying. Please don't fall for it. Continue to stand your ground and make your plans. Work on building your strength and self-esteem. There is light at the end of this tunnel.

# Chapter 15:
# Preparing to Leave

*"First ask yourself: What is the worst that can happen? Then prepare to accept it. Then proceed to improve on the worst."*

—Dale Carnegie

Whether you're ready to walk out the door today or you need some time to get stronger before you leave, there are many practical actions you'll need to take to ensure the split isn't any bumpier than it has to be. Many of these preparations you'll need to handle *before* you advise your partner or spouse you are leaving.

Please be aware that throughout this entire process, you may feel conflicted and afraid. You've spent years being emotionally trampled on and worn down to a nub. You've been toeing the line for your spouse and jumping when he or she says, "Jump." Now you're about to step out and do what your abuser considers unthinkable—leave.

Even if your mind is saying, "Get the hell out," your psyche might be screaming, "What the hell are you doing?" Just try to keep putting one foot in front of the other, taking small daily actions to move the process forward.

Here are some of the actions you'll need to handle as part of the preparation process. Most of this information relates to those who are married to their abusers, but I'll also cover ideas for those cohabiting.

**Gather any and all documentation of abuse** to you and your children. If you don't have any, start collecting it now. Write down and date every incident, and take photos or video, if possible. Keep this documentation in a safe place where your spouse can't find it. Make a copy and keep it somewhere outside your house.

**Start gathering all the financial information you can.** If your spouse controls the finances, this may be difficult, but collect what you can. The court system will require your spouse to turn over a financial statement, if you can't collect anything.

You'll want to know your assets, debts, investments, possessions, available cash, monthly expenses, and income. If you can get your hands on a few years' worth of tax returns, make copies and keep them in a safe place. If you are cohabiting and some items in the house belong to you, make plans to move them out shortly before or on the day you talk with your partner.

**Research and retain a respected divorce attorney.** Create a list of questions and call several before setting an appointment. Get as much answered over the phone as possible, so you don't have to pay for a consult with someone you may not use.

Your budget may dictate the attorney you use, but, if at all possible, have your own attorney rather than sharing one with your spouse or using a mediator. You want someone focused on your best interests. If you're not married, but you own a house jointly, you'll need an attorney to help you determine the best course of action for getting your money out of the house.

**Be sure to tell the attorney about the emotional abuse.** Share any documentation, share your financial documents, and let the attorney know what you hope to achieve in the way of child support, custody, division of assets, and alimony (if applicable). Your attorney should have a good idea of what you can expect, given your circumstances and financial situation.

**Discuss with your attorney what the best temporary separation arrangement** should be. In some states, it isn't advisable to leave your house, as it might be viewed as abandonment. However, if your spouse won't leave, you may need to consider this. Once you tell your partner it's over, things may escalate, and you'll need to get out quickly.

**Have a plan for where you'll go, whether it's a temporary or permanent place to live**. You may need to go through the court system for a temporary separation agreement that spells out exactly the terms of separation and a temporary custody arrangement. If you stay in the house, call a locksmith to change the locks.

**Be sure you have enough cash for a couple of months,** especially if you don't have access to your checking account or you fear your partner may cut you off or cancel credit cards. If you work, ask that your paycheck be sent to a post office box or given to you directly, so it isn't intercepted or put into a joint account. If you are not married but share finances and have a joint account, remove the money that is yours and put it in a separate account. Do this shortly before you tell your partner about the breakup, so it doesn't alert him or her to your plans.

**Grab and compile any important documents for you and your kids,** such as birth certificates, social security numbers, insurance cards, passports, etc. Make copies of any other important documents that you can't remove from the house.

**Begin planning how you can support yourself once you are divorced,** especially if you are concerned about your ability to afford living on your own, and you don't anticipate alimony or child support. You may need to further your education, learn a new skill, look for a job or a better job, or get a loan from family or a friend to set yourself up.

You might decide you need to live with a friend or relative temporarily while you get your feet on the ground. This is the time to talk with friends and family about various resources, networks, and options for you once you leave. Just be sure that no one you discuss your plans with leaks them to your partner.

**Consider how the divorce will impact your children and what you'll need to do to ease their way through it.** You may need to arrange counseling for them, prepare to move them to a new school, and talk with their teachers and school counselor about the changes that are about to happen. You need to have a plan in mind about how and when you will tell the children about the breakup, whether or not your partner is included, how much you want to tell them, and how you will handle their grief and pain. Your counselor can help you sort through these issues.

**A few days prior to breaking the news to your partner, have an emergency bag packed for you and the kids.** Be sure your car is filled with gas, your phone is charged and on your body, and you have all your important documents in a safe place out of the house. You may not need this, but if the conversation goes badly, you'll be glad you're prepared.

**Consider getting a new phone number after your breakup,** and decide how you want to advise the necessary people in your life about this change. You may have friends as couples, coworkers, employees, neighbors, and others whom you will need to inform.

**One of the most important things you need to prepare for is how your partner will react when you break the news.** It's important that you prepare mentally and emotionally by anticipating his or her possible reactions. Your partner may try any one or several of these tactics to punish you or get you to stay.

- Make promises that he or she intends to change and stop the abuse.

- Threaten you financially, physically, or by implying you'll be punished in some other way.

- Undermine your self-esteem by attacking your ability to survive, your appearance, or your desirability to anyone else.

- Attempt to isolate you from friends and family members.

- Attempt to manipulate you with guilt trips, shaming, blame, or histrionics.

All the tactics your abuser has used during the relationship will likely get thrown against the wall to see what sticks. Prepare yourself for these tactics and expect them. You can better prepare yourself by having a few strategies for dealing with your abuser's behavior.

**If possible, have a support person with you** when you break the news. You might consider announcing your plans in a counseling session, or have a friend or family member in the house with you.

**Prepare a clear, concise statement you'll make to your partner** and rehearse it. You might say something like, "Our relationship is broken, and I see no way to fix it. I will no longer accept being in an abusive relationship. I have made a firm decision to divorce (or end the relationship) and have begun taking steps toward that."

**If things start to get heated, be prepared to leave the house with your support person.** Your spouse will probably protest, question you, or get angry and walk away. If you do stay and talk, keep the conversation to a minimum and don't allow yourself to be sucked into your partner's abusive tactics or looping accusations or begging. Stand firm.

**After you have the initial conversation with your spouse or partner, but within a few days, present any necessary documents,** next steps, or suggest he or she gets an attorney. Implement your plan for temporary separation with your attorney's advice as soon as possible.

This will be an extremely difficult time for you, and you'll have moments when you want to change your mind simply to escape the pain and discomfort. Just remind yourself of all the work you've done to get to this point.

Stay in regular contact with your counselor and other support people. Ask them to remind you why you are in this situation and your determination to leave. Try to remember you are doing the best for your long-term mental health, happiness, and maybe even your physical safety.

If you have children, remember you are being a good role model to them by showing them that emotional abuse is unacceptable and by removing them from this dynamic between you and your partner. You will have a deluge of emotions, but this is the time to trust your judgment rather than your feelings. Keep moving forward with strength and self-assurance.

# Chapter 16:
# Preparing Your Children

*"I strongly believe children can thrive through divorce. Children need parents who love them. Children need to know they are safe. Children need stability and sometimes that's much easier to achieve outside a marriage than in a broken one."*

—Lisa Hayes

Telling your children you are ending the marriage or relationship with their other parent is gut-wrenching. There's no other word for it, but it must be done. The question is, how can you discuss this with your children without making this already painful time even more painful?

It's optimal if you and your spouse can sit down together with your kids to discuss the breakup. If your partner generally has a good relationship with your children and hasn't shown he or she wants to make you suffer in front of them, try to arrange a time together to talk with them.

However, this may not be possible if you fear your abusive partner may blow up or cause a scene in front of your children. Also if you suspect he or she will blame you or attempt to undermine your relationship with your children, you should probably talk to your kids without your spouse.

## What Do You Say?

So what exactly do you say to your children, and when do you say it? A lot will depend on how old your children are and how much they can understand.

If you have children of varying ages, you may want to tell them separately, as they will have differing questions and need different amounts of information.

It's important to talk with them during a calm time that isn't rushed. Don't do it immediately after a fight with your spouse that they can hear, during homework time, just before school, or right before they go to bed. A weekend morning might be a good time to allow them to process, ask questions, and deal with grief and tears before they go back to school or try to fall asleep.

If you and your partner are talking to them together, try to show as much respect and compassion for your partner as you can during the conversation. In fact, the more respectful you can act toward your partner in front of your kids, even if he or she is behaving badly, the easier it will be for your children to cope.

When you let your kids know you want to have a talk, they may already suspect that divorce or separation is imminent. Children have an uncanny way of picking up on the vibe of the household, even if you've done a great job of keeping your plans under wraps.

Start the conversation by acknowledging you have something difficult to discuss, and that you both love them very much. Then simply say the words, "Your dad and I (or your mom and I) are not happy together and can't live together any more. We have mutually decided we need to separate (or divorce), and we want to talk with you about it."

Let them know it's a mutual decision, even if it isn't. This may be difficult for your abusive partner to agree to, but it's really better for your kids not to think one of you is the "bad guy" in the decision.

If your partner states that he or she doesn't want the breakup, then acknowledge this as true, but remind your kids that the marriage is broken, and it's causing you too much pain to stay together.

Let your children know clearly that both of you will always be there for them and love them the same, regardless of what's happening between you and your partner.

Be sure to reinforce that they are not at fault for your decision in any way. Say something like, "Nothing you did caused this to happen. This happened because of adult problems between us that have nothing to do with anything you've said or done."

Invite questions from your kids and validate their feelings of sadness, confusion, or anger. But you do not need to share any other details about the reason for the breakup other than to say the marriage is broken and you can't stay together.

## Show Restraint

Children, even teenagers, don't need to know all the adult reasons behind your decision, and as tempting as it might be to blame your abusive spouse, don't do it. Unless your spouse is abusing your kids, you need to allow your children to have a good relationship with both of you without feeling the need to choose sides.

Your kids may continue to ask about the reasons behind the divorce, but gently and firmly let them know that you will not be telling them. Be consistent with this, as they may continue to ask even after several conversations. Older children and teenagers especially will want answers and may even seek to blame one of you.

It takes a great deal of restraint and maturity for you to hold this boundary, but it is truly in the best interest of your children and frees them from the unnecessary responsibility of trying to sort out adult decisions.

If your children have witnessed the emotional abuse in your home or have been victims of the abuse themselves, they may ask you if this is the cause for the breakup. If you deny the abuse, that will only make your children question themselves, so simply acknowledge that the abuse was part of the decision.

But remember that anything critical you say about your spouse reverberates in your children's hearts. You are speaking about part of whom they are, so a negative judgment of your spouse also implicitly becomes a criticism of them.

Both you and your children may cry during this conversation. They may become angry and yell at you or storm out of the room. Let them know you accept their emotions, and that they are free to express all their feelings with you at any time. But try not to burden your children with your emotions.

Let your children know that any sadness they see in you has nothing to do with them and that you are strong and will be OK. Try to be calm in discussions and don't make your kids your confidants. They are not adults and shouldn't have to shoulder the additional pain of supporting you.

Your children need some level of assurance that despite this dramatic and painful life event, they will be OK and both their parents (or at least one of them) are confident, mature adults who will put their interests first.

Let them know you and your spouse want to make the process as calm and respectful as possible, and that both of you are strong enough to face whatever comes your way. You may not feel this way in the moment, but do your best to let your children see strength and emotional maturity.

# The Practical Changes to Expect

Once you have let your children know your plans and offered them comfort, share some of the practical changes they can anticipate.

Let them know where they will live, how often they will see both parents, and any other changes they should expect. If you aren't sure about something yet, tell them that you'll keep them informed as soon as you have the answers.

Again, reassure your children that you will always love them, and even though you and your partner are ending your relationship, neither of you will ever end the relationship with them.

Say something like, "No matter what, we love you very much. The kind of love we have for you is the kind that never ends. We will always be your parents, and we will continue to take care of you."

Try your best to minimize tension and anger in your home as you go through the separation and divorce process, while maintaining your boundaries with your spouse or partner. This will be a difficult time for everyone, but your children are innocent in this process and deserve as much support, continuity, and reassurance as you can offer.

Keep the lines of communication open with them, and respond to their pain as honestly as you can. You may feel guilty for putting your children through this pain, but remember you are working toward creating a more peaceful, loving environment for yourself and for them. In the long run, this is one of the best gifts you can give them.

Barrie Davenport

# Chapter 17:
# Still Conflicted after the Split

*"I don't miss him; I miss who I thought he was."*

—Unknown

You've had the courage and strength to leave your abusive spouse, or maybe you're in the midst of ending the relationship. But you still feel stuck and conflicted about your decision.

Now that you've acknowledged the abuse and recognized that it likely won't change, there's still a part of you that loves your partner and feels despondent at the thought of no longer being with this person.

This is a perfectly normal and expected reaction. If you've been with your spouse for years, you've shared a life together, and maybe have children together, you've developed deep and strong roots that are intertwined. Untangling these emotional connections takes time and perspective.

In addition to the normal bonds any long-term couple develops, you've been trained or even brainwashed to believe you have no identity outside of what your abuser offers you. You've lost your sense of self, so leaving your abuser may feel like part of you is actually dying.

## Reframing Your Pain

Perhaps a better way to reframe this feeling is by viewing the pain you feel as the pain of rebirth rather than death. You are being reborn into the person you really are. But as long as you cling to the old relationship, in thought or in reality, you're preventing yourself from being reborn and claiming your authentic self.

You may find yourself stuck in a mental loop of "what ifs" and "maybe I'm doing the wrong thing," and suddenly all the good times and positive qualities of your abusive partner are spotlighted in your thoughts. You ruminate over and over, and as much as you know intellectually you need to move on, you just can't seem to let go.

Dr. Tara Palmatier, a therapist who works with couples in emotionally abusive relationships, says this on her relationship site:

> If you're stuck on an abusive ex or still in a relationship with an abusive partner, but can't break free because you "love" her, you need to wake up. The abusive ex or partner is not some irreplaceable, special snowflake. She or he is not the end all be all—I don't care how good the sex is or how good the sex was. She is not your soul

*mate. She is not the one. She is not your destiny, unless you believe that you're fated to spend your life in misery. In reality, you're probably not hung up on her, but on old childhood wounds and the fantasies you have built around her that have nothing to do with who she is in reality. Most likely, she represents a chance at a new outcome to an old hurt.*

If you are stuck like this, it is likely a sign you have more work to do on your unfinished business from the past. You are grieving the loss of acceptance and approval from your original abuser as much as the loss of your partner.

You are still trying to work out a fantasy you've created with your partner that rights all the wrongs you experienced as a child. Unfortunately, your partner isn't playing the role of the handsome prince or the beautiful princess who will live happily ever after.

As much as you might torment yourself with second guessing, what-ifs, and fantasy dreams, you'll never be able to love, cajole, or understand your partner enough so he'll treat you well and offer you healthy love. You can't save or fix this person, and you shouldn't waste time trying. Once you accept that, you have the key to your own emotional freedom.

Barrie Davenport

# Pay Attention to Actions

An important thing to remember when you're in this stuck place is that actions always speak louder than words. So pay attention to the former and current actions of your partner and your feelings when you are around him or her—not what you want them to be, but what they truly are.

If things haven't changed by now, they won't. You wouldn't be in this position if your partner didn't exhibit consistent abusive behaviors, and you didn't constantly feel wounded by them. As the poet Maya Angelou says, "When someone shows you who they are, believe them the first time."

If you intellectually accept this is true, you need to exert the self-discipline to change your mindset. As harsh as it may sound, you need to kick your conflicted emotions to the curb and redirect your thoughts to something truly productive or distracting when those thoughts try to invade your mind.

Give yourself a good shake when your "but I love him (or her)" feelings arise, and remind yourself you're grieving the loss of your hopes and dreams, not reality.

Remember too that when you indulge in conflicted thinking, you're ripping the scabs off wounds that are trying to heal. Leave them be and allow yourself to heal until you are strong enough to see your abusive partner in the clear light of day.

You may need to redirect your thoughts a hundred times a day in the beginning, but keep doing it, and trust your good judgment and all the work you've done to get to this place.

You're not crazy.

You're not selfish.

You're not unloving.

You're not wrong.

You are here because you are the victim of emotional abuse, and you're not going to take it any longer.

Barrie Davenport

# Chapter 18:
# Rebuilding Self-Esteem and Confidence

*"Never bend your head. Always hold it high.
Look the world straight in the eye."*

—Helen Keller

There was a time in my life when I didn't believe in myself. Having grown up in your average dysfunctional family, I found myself in the role of peacekeeper and people pleaser from a young age.

I believed if I was compliant and accommodating, I could keep everyone happy and prevent the crazy-making behavior going on around me. On a deeper level, I was afraid of being emotionally abandoned. When my efforts didn't work, I tried harder.

Needless to say, over time I trained myself to stuff down my own feelings, for fear I'd rock the boat further and lose the love I had.
This is the role I also played in my adult relationships. It's the role that felt normal, because as a child, I didn't have any other coping strategies.

So as an adult, I simply repeated what I knew and applied it to my relationships.

During confrontational situations as an adult, I either backed down quickly or avoided engaging altogether. Although I was "rewarded" for being a pleaser, eventually my self-esteem began to waiver. I had false beliefs that I wasn't good enough if I didn't comply to the wants and needs of others. As you know, this mindset was unsustainable and soul crushing.

When you get to this point, your psyche—and sometimes your body—begin to revolt. My internal revolution burst forth as raging generalized anxiety, accompanied by weird, unexplainable physical pains.

Fortunately, with the help of a caring counselor, I was able to break free from these self-destructive beliefs and behaviors to know exactly what I want and deserve for myself.

Whether you've decided to leave your abusive relationship or stay together, you need to rebuild your self-esteem to live a full and happy life. Self-esteem is essential for being a fully actualized individual.

When we don't love ourselves, we compromise our relationships and every other part of our lives. We simply can't function at an optimal level and fulfill our potential for happiness and success.

As an emotional abuse victim, you've probably forgotten how to trust yourself and rely on your own beliefs and judgments. Instead you may look to others to build you up and manufacture your self-esteem.

As an abuse victim, it's easy to get trapped in the negativity bias, an evolutionary adaptation in which we pay much more attention to negative beliefs and events than positive. We are simply wired to focus more on our flaws and shortcomings than on our positive qualities.

When your flaws have been reinforced by your partner and by your parents and others throughout your life, the negativity bias has been further reinforced and entrenched in your mind. You've created a lifelong pattern of self-criticism and self-doubt that is hard to escape.

To embrace your true worthiness, you'll need to learn new ways of self-talk and responding to the input you receive from the world around you.

This is something you will have to work at, because you've had years of sabotaging beliefs undermining your self-esteem. If you've made the decision to no longer accept emotional abuse in your life, then the next step is making the decision to reclaim your self-worth and learn to love yourself. This requires some daily, even hourly, self-work to learn a new way of thinking and acting.

## 1. Define worthiness for yourself.

Create your own personal operating system for life, without relying on what others think is best for you.

Examine your own values and define your integrity. Get clear on what you believe, rather than what your spouse or partner has made you believe.

What kind of person do you want to be? How do you want to live your life within the context of what is realistically attainable?

## 2. Become aware of your thoughts.

Start paying attention to the nature of your thoughts and how often you think negative, critical things about yourself. This awareness alone will help you disengage from the thoughts, if only for a few minutes.

Diminish the reality and power of your negative thoughts by identifying and detaching from them. Say something to yourself like, "There are those negative thoughts again. Look at what they are doing to me. They don't reflect who I really am."

## 3. Filter your perceptions.

Remind yourself that many of these critical thoughts have their origin in the words or actions of your partner or original abuser, but are they really true?

As you become more aware of your thinking patterns, begin to filter your thoughts by applying the light of reality to them. Ask yourself, "Is my thought really the truth? Is it the entire truth or just my perception of the truth?"

Challenge all your negative thoughts, and seek evidence that contradicts your negative beliefs. Do what you can to loosen your grasp on self-limiting beliefs.

## 4. Create new environments.

If certain environments or situations highlight or reinforce your feelings of low self-worth, change your environment. You may not be able to leave your home, but try to put yourself in situations more often where you feel successful, confident, accepted, and happy.

Play to your strengths, and focus on your natural aptitudes rather than struggling against something or someone who constantly brings you down.

If you still live with your abusive partner out of necessity, try spending more time with supportive family and friends and less time with your partner, if possible. Go for long walks, get involved in a hobby, or join a group that is enjoyable and relaxing.

## 5. Practice realistic optimism.

When you really don't believe you're lovable, affirming that you are lovable feels false. Rather than making blanket statements about your self-worth, identify more honest, but optimistic, affirmations you can say to yourself.

For example, you might say, "Today I'm not as confident as I want to be, but I know I can improve and feel better about myself."

173

Improvement is always possible, and working on an improvement goal will make you feel better about yourself. Improving your self-esteem and confidence will take some time, so be patient with yourself.

## 6. Learn the power of acceptance.

Maybe you don't like your physical appearance. Maybe you aren't the funniest or most engaging person in your circle. You might look at other people and long to be like them.

There are some realities in life that are genetic, that you had no control over, or that will never change. You can struggle against them or learn to give yourself as much acceptance and understanding as you have the abusive people in your life.

By accepting yourself, you free your energy to focus on other more productive, positive endeavors. You practice acceptance by facing your flaws honestly and simply choosing to like yourself anyway.

If positive change is possible, then do whatever you can to change your behaviors, choices, and actions to support your feelings of self-love.

Just remember that outward change alone won't make you feel more lovable. You'll feel better about yourself for taking action, but that action must be supported with inner work on your thoughts and beliefs.

## 7. Celebrate your unique qualities.

Sometimes what we criticize about ourselves is considered our best, most unique quality by others.

If you were the black sheep of your family, you might believe you are the "odd" one. But as an adult, other people regard your personality or lifestyle as interesting and attractive.

Don't strive to fit in or conform to your abuser's desires for who you should be. Celebrate being unique.

## 8. Practice gratitude.

During the times when you catch yourself in negative thinking, switch gears entirely and focus on gratitude. Make a list of everything you are grateful for in your life—from the most insignificant to the most important.

Don't just jot things down quickly. Really focus on each item on the list, and think about how you'd feel without it. Study after study has shown that the regular practice of gratitude helps improve your outlook and feelings of happiness.

## 9. Show compassion for yourself.

Pretend you are your own best friend, and show the kind of compassion to yourself you would show to someone you care about.

Rather than putting yourself down, use words of encouragement and support. You are as deserving of kindness as anyone, so set the stage for that by treating yourself kindly.

Set realistic goals for yourself, and avoid the perfectionist syndrome of assuming you are all bad unless you do everything perfectly.

## 10. Learn healthy communication skills.

Being able to communicate your feelings and fears in mature, nonconfrontational, healthy ways is critical to self-esteem and improved relationships.

Everyone has insecurities, but rather than hide or diminish them, improve your emotional intelligence so you are less reactive and more authentic. This may not be possible with your emotionally abusive partner, but you have many other relationships in your life in which you can practice these skills.

Do some research on healthy communication and emotional intelligence so you can learn how to practice the skills.

## 11. Be willing to set boundaries.

We discussed forming boundaries with your partner earlier in the book, but it's worth reinforcing here. If you've allowed your partner and other people to cross your boundaries, it's going to take a determined effort on your part to set them and stick to them.

Decide how you want to be treated and what you will and won't tolerate. Start by communicating one new boundary at a time and practice holding firm with it.

## 12. Speak up for yourself.

Part of creating and following through on your boundaries is learning to speak up for yourself. If others say or do things you don't like, or if you have ideas or input you previously held back for fear of offending someone, try stepping out of your comfort zone and speaking your mind. You can do this calmly but decisively, even if you have to pretend at first.

## 13. Take care of yourself.

You show love and compassion for yourself when you treat your body, mind, and emotions with care. That means eating healthy foods, exercising, getting enough sleep, going to the doctor, taking care of your hygiene, having a support system, and finding ways to stimulate your mind. When you treat yourself as someone with value, you'll feel more valuable.

## 14. Practice forgiveness.

To love yourself, you must first forgive yourself and forgive others who have hurt you. You forgive yourself in the same way you forgive a loved one who genuinely seeks forgiveness. You offer it freely with compassion.

Beating yourself up over and over again is an exercise in futility. Do what needs to be done to right any wrongs and regain your integrity, and then let it go.

If others have wounded you, offer the same forgiveness to them—even if they don't seek it. The ability to forgive is a huge step toward self-respect and wholeness.

Forgiving someone doesn't mean you accept their behaviors or will allow them to be repeated. It simply means you have let go of the anger and hurt so it doesn't destroy your life.

## 15. Simplify and create balance.

A complicated, overly scheduled life, coupled with an abusive relationship, drains your energy and creates anxiety. Decide how much order and balance you want in your life, and begin cutting back on the tasks, obligations, and material things that don't add to your life.

This will give you breathing room to work on yourself, heal from your abuse, and redefine how you want to spend your time and energy. Giving yourself this space is a way of showing love to yourself.

## 16. Stop comparing yourself to others.

Many people who have been emotionally abused spend too much time comparing themselves to other people. Because they don't have an inherent sense of self-worth, they look to others to give themselves a measuring stick.

This means their self-esteem is completely dependent on whether or not they see themselves as better or worse than other people. Rather than comparing, try to acknowledge the differences you have with others without placing a value judgment on it or seeing yourself as inferior.

## 17. Continue to deal with past wounds.

If emotional abuse from your childhood or more recent past has impacted your self-esteem and restricted your ability to love yourself, then continue to take action to heal those wounds.

I want to reinforce the importance of finding a good professional counselor who can help you navigate through the past pain and work with you to learn new ways of relating to yourself and others.

Once you break free of an emotionally abusive relationship or find a way to manage the abuse, you may have the overwhelming desire to just move on and shove all the pain and emotional effort under the rug. You're probably so tired of dealing with it, that you just want to live your life and enjoy yourself in peace.

But if you don't change your mindset and internal reference, you're bound to repeat the patterns of self-sabotaging behaviors in your next relationship or to allow your current relationship to slip back into old patterns.

The work on yourself must continue, so that you rebuild yourself from the inside out, creating a firm foundation of confidence and self-esteem to move on to a happy and successful life.

# Chapter 19:
# Embracing Personal Responsibility

*"Don't rely on someone else for your happiness and self-worth. Only you can be responsible for that. If you can't love and respect yourself—no one else will be able to make that happen."*

—Stacey Charter

You have a variety of reasons for living in an emotionally abusive relationship and suffering the loss of self-esteem and confidence as a result. There is no doubt you have been treated poorly, not only in your love relationship, but perhaps also in your childhood.

You have many painful feelings related to your abuse and your responses to it, feelings that make you want to retreat and avoid addressing your own baggage and victim behaviors. You have many entrenched beliefs and behaviors that are difficult obstacles to overcome.

Sometimes it seems so much easier just to accept life as is and operate within the confines of what feels expected and comfortable. It's easier to barricade yourself with excuses, blame, guilt, and fear and bury your head in the sand.

Ultimately, however, your happiness and emotional well-being is in your own hands—no matter how much pain you've endured.

This requires addressing the causes for your choices and behaviors and actively practicing the skills you've learned to rebuild your self-esteem and make empowered choices moving forward.

You have made a huge leap in your awareness and self-esteem. Hopefully you no longer back down when your partner abuses you. You no longer accept learned helplessness or fear-based reactions. Simply by reading this book, you have empowered yourself.

The essence of self-empowerment is personal responsibility—taking full and complete control and accountability for your own life and circumstances. This is both liberating and scary.

It's liberating because taking full responsibility for your life means you:

- Make your own choices and decisions.

- Live according to your own personal operating system and values.

- Free yourself from the anxiety of living up to the expectations of others.

- Experience the joy of being authentically yourself.

But it's frightening because you:

- Might make your abuser's behavior escalate and make life more difficult in the short term.

- Can no longer blame others for your failures and disappointments.

- Can't cling to childish, dependent security from others.

- Have to let go of the "old you," even if that person was holding you back.

However, as you empower yourself through personal responsibility, those fears begin to dissipate. You find your self-confidence soars, things are easier, and life is more enjoyable, because you are creating it on your own terms rather than reacting to your fears or outside circumstances.

Relinquishing responsibility for your life, to your abuser or anyone else, means you are giving away your power through fear and blaming. You are allowing the winds of fate to rule you and resigning yourself to a compromised life.

The more you do this, the more your self-esteem suffers. It's hard to respect yourself when you allow your old patterns and fears to hold you back from your potential.

## Rewriting Your Story

So how can you step up to your personal responsibility and empower yourself?

First, examine yourself and take a hard look at your life right now to see where you might be giving away your power.

How are you letting other people, including your partner, define or control you or your behavior?

Who are you blaming for your life problems?

What are you avoiding and what excuses are you giving yourself and others?

Next, kill the victim mentality. You have been a victim, but you don't need to remain one. Self-empowered people don't see themselves as victims. They view themselves as creators, survivors, and thrivers. To take control of your own life and nurture happy relationships in the future, you must let go of your past victim mentality.

You may not even recognize that you embrace a victim mentality. It could be deeply entrenched in your psyche from being victimized in the past. Sometimes it even feels good to be a victim, because it brings sympathy and attention. But that's all you get from it. Sympathy and attention aren't enough for a confident, happy life.

Part of being a victim involves perpetuating a "story" about yourself that you repeat to explain why you are who you are, why you can't take action for change, and why you behave the way you do. All of us have these stories, and they are based in some truth. You had a bad childhood. Your spouse is unloving. You only attract abusive people in your life.

But if you allow these situations to be the constant backdrop for your life, you will never escape being the leading character of a sad story. The more you reinforce your story, the more entrenched you become in it. The key is stepping out of the old story and rewriting a new one that puts you in the driver's seat of your life.

I'm not trying to diminish the real pain, fear, and difficulty involved in ending emotional abuse. The feelings of being stuck, powerless, hopeless, and unsupported can be overwhelming and at times insurmountable.

Embracing personal responsibility for your life doesn't happen overnight. You have to practice but also be kind and patient with yourself. You need to do the things that self-empowered people do until you gain mastery and confidence.

# Changing Your Language

Begin by simply shifting your thoughts away from victim language and toward success language. Assert yourself in your relationship, even if you can't leave it right now or don't see hope for any lasting change.

Try to catch yourself in thoughts of blame, shame, guilt, or self-pity. Then replace those thoughts with words of confidence, gratitude, self-love, and acceptance. Begin supporting your new thinking with action.

Where you once said, "I can't. I'm too weak. I'm too afraid," take one small action in the direction of "I can!" Every small action will empower you.

Contrary to popular belief, taking personal responsibility for your life often means embracing positive support from other people. Asking for help does not mean you are weak or incapable.

It means you are empowered enough to take full responsibility for your own personal evolution. It means you are seeking just another way to expedite your awareness, self-esteem, and knowledge.

This help can come in the form of books, courses, therapy, coaching, and the counsel of friends and family. Everyone, even the most self-confident, can benefit from the support and insights of others who have our best interests at heart.

In fact, I highly recommend you continue with counseling until you feel strong enough to settle for nothing less than an equal, mutually respectful, healthy relationship.

As this book comes to a close, remember that you alone are ultimately responsible for your life and happiness. You CAN improve your circumstances, assert your needs and boundaries, and change the way you feel about yourself as you practice the techniques outlined in this book.

But no one else can make you practice. No one else can push you past the feelings of fear, doubt, and discomfort to take action on ending the abuse in your life and moving forward on your own terms. Every day you must reclaim your personal power by taking the necessary actions to improve your situation.

With every empowered action you take toward healing and reclaiming yourself, you will see how profoundly your efforts have paid off as you feel more and more sure of yourself and your worthiness to enjoy a loving, happy relationship.

Although your recovery from your abusive relationship will take time, you will be rewarded for your courage and determination all along the way. There is joy and peace on the other side of abuse, and it's yours to claim.

Barrie Davenport

# Chapter 20:
# The Dynamics of a
# Healthy Relationship

*"A loving relationship is one in which the loved
one is free to be himself—to laugh with me,
but never at me; to cry with me,
but never because of me; to love life,
to love himself, to love being loved. Such a
relationship is based upon freedom and can
never grow in a jealous heart."*

—Leo Buscaglia

Despite your past or current experience of
emotional abuse, research confirms that being in a
relationship is a really good thing. People who are
in a committed relationship live longer, are happier
in general, and tend to accumulate more wealth.

But if that's the case, why are relationships so
difficult? Why do we abuse, belittle, and disengage
from the one person we're supposed to love most?

I find it ironic that we go through extensive training
to drive a car and spend years in school to prepare

for a career, but there is no expected or required training when it comes to the most important part of our lives—our love relationship.

No one teaches us how to be a good partner and how to nurture the health of the relationship. No one tells us how our past wounds and life experiences might impact our choice of a partner and how we should relate to a partner who treats us badly.

To move forward with a healthy, new relationship or to heal your current one, you need to know what a healthy, satisfying connection looks like and what it takes from both partners to create this special dynamic.

One of my blog readers who was emotionally abused was able to leave her abusive partner and is beginning to seek a new relationship. She says:

> My biggest challenge now is that I want to know what I can do going forward into new relationships to NOT attract men who will become abusive. If there is something that I did to attract this type, I want to know. If there is something that I can do to spot early warning signs, I want to know.
>
> What I have figured out so far is that real love is based on intimacy (closeness/connectedness) and respect. I see now that in my previous abusive relationship, we never really connected.

A relationship itself is a living, breathing thing that must be nurtured and cared for daily—above our own individual needs or frustrations. It you want your relationship to work, you both must work at your relationship. It can't be one-sided, and it can't be neglected.

By prioritizing the relationship, you are working as a unit rather than as two wounded individuals trying to use the other to get your emotional needs met.

What if couples were able to willingly admit their needs and inner wounds, and empathize with each other, fostering a type of "positive dependency"—a loving, safe environment in which each supports and nurtures the other?

## The Couple Bubble

This idea has been explored in depth by a number of couple therapists, such as Dr. Stan Tatkin, who has labeled it "the couple bubble." Essentially, this means that the couple commit to placing their relationship first and foremost, creating a place of reassurance and protection.

Mutuality takes the place of autonomy. Encouragement and support take the place of threats and guilt. Unlike codependency, in which the relationship is driven by insecurity and fear, the couple bubble is driven by empathy, understanding, and acceptance.

Within the couple bubble, dependency becomes a strength, rather than a weakness. A couple in a couple bubble will know that, come what may, they have each other's backs. They feel the peace and contentment that comes from knowing that they are cherished and safe. They are two against the world, and as a team they are indestructible.

There are no secrets, no judgments, and no insecurities within the couple bubble. It is as warm and as protective as your own home.
In his book, *Wired for Love*, Stan Tatkin has defined the couple bubble as based on a series of agreements, such as:

> *I will never leave you.*

> *I will never frighten you purposely.*

> *When you are in distress, I will relieve you, even if I'm the one who is causing the distress.*

> *You will be the first to hear about anything and not the second, third, or fourth person I tell.*
>
> —Stan Tatkin, *Wired for Love*, p. 12

These agreements are consciously held—like a pact. Above all, you are saying to each other: "We come first."

Each of you need to become an expert on your partner.

- What makes your partner feel safe and secure, above all else?

- What will upset him or her?

- What will reassure your partner?

Of course, no one can expect to be a perfect partner at all times. There will be occasions when you do hurt your partner, even unintentionally. The key here is to make amends as quickly as possible.

Don't let a situation fester when it becomes lodged in the long-term memory and may be difficult to release. Address a leak in your couple bubble right away. Hold up your hands and apologize, talk about it, and be sure there are no lasting hard feelings.

It helps to build a repository of positive, happy memories and experiences to counteract the effect of the odd negative, sad blow. We tend to retain negative memories for longer and with more clarity than we do positive ones—so it makes sense to fill up on loving gestures whenever possible.

Learn what makes your partner feel good, and act on it. Hug your partner often, send affectionate messages, make breakfast in bed for long, lazy mornings. It's the little things that count.

Let each other know that whatever happens, you're there for each other. If your partner is distressed or needs help, you should be the first person to whom he or she turns. No issue is too weighty or trivial. Accept that within the couple bubble, you can be vulnerable—your partner is your rock!

When you create a couple bubble, there's no room for emotional abuse, manipulation, or control.

Let's look at some characteristics of a healthy relationship that are protected by a couple bubble.

## 1. You make the relationship your top priority.

There is no doubt, your marriage or partnership is THE most valuable part of your life. If it's not, it should be. It should come before your work, hobbies, extended family, and, yes—even before your children.

As a couple, you are the centerpiece of your family, and if the couple isn't strong, the family isn't strong.

Both partners must be committed to putting the relationship as their top life priority. This can't be just empty words. It has to be acknowledged between the two of you and demonstrated in your daily, even hourly, commitment to keeping the relationship healthy and thriving.

## 2. You communicate openly and regularly.

You make it a habit to check in with each other every day or every few days to get a pulse on your connection. Both people feel safe and free to express concerns, disappointments, and frustrations, and both of you feel motivated to find resolution or seek compromise when necessary.

You each express your feelings kindly and directly, without using passive-aggressive behavior, manipulation, or stonewalling. You don't hold things back or shove them away to avoid confrontation.

In fact, confrontation isn't part of your communication style. You are driven to get things back on track because of your love for each other and your deep value of the relationship itself.

## 3. You create emotional intimacy.

Emotional intimacy is the closeness you share together. You feel free and secure to express your fears and vulnerabilities without being shamed or demeaned. You have a high level of trust, transparency, and openness between you, based on your love for each other and the years of shared experiences.

Emotionally intimate couples can share their deepest selves and are able to express the depth of their feelings for each other. In this context, each person feels wholly accepted, respected, and worthy in the eyes of their partner.

Emotional intimacy can be fostered by becoming more familiar with your own feelings, needs, fears, and desires. You must be self-aware to be intimate with another person. Emotional intimacy also requires that you spend quality time with your partner together, away from daily stress and distractions.

## 4. You create sexual intimacy.

Emotional intimacy is the foundation for a healthy sexual relationship, and the combination creates a deep bond between two people. When you have emotional intimacy, you are free to express what you desire sexually—and you are free to give fully to the other person.

Sex is not just a physical pleasure or release, but rather an expression of your deep love and closeness. Emotional intimacy makes room for play, exploration, and complete safety in the bedroom.

You can still have sexual experiences with each other that are primarily physical, but you can do so with the security of the deep emotional connection you share.

## 5. You spend time together.

You can't nurture the relationship without spending time together. This is more than just being in the same house together or spending time together with children.

You need to prioritize time for just the two of you. You need the space to enjoy each other's company, to share interests and experiences, and to simply have fun.

Many relationships fall apart because the couple is basically living separate lives. Each person has his or her own interests and obligations, and simply don't make time to be together.

They allow the demands of life to fill their hours, and then over time, they realize they have nothing in common and little to say to each other.

## 6. You speak kindly.

The words and tone of voice you use with your spouse or partner has a profound impact, as you know from experience. Neither of you want to sound detached, irritated, sarcastic, or demeaning in a loving relationship.

If you cherish this person, then speak to him or her in ways that reflect that. It's so easy to take the other person for granted and to lash out when you're feeling stressed or overwhelmed. If you do this enough, your words create deep wounds and undermine the intimacy of the relationship.

Simply speak kindly to the person you love. Your words have more power than you can possibly imagine.

## 7. You are affectionate with each other.

Non-sexual touch, such as hugging, holding hands, kissing, and cuddling, is vital to a healthy relationship. Studies have shown that couples who enjoy regular physical affection tend to be happier and more satisfied with their relationship. They also recover more quickly from conflict.

Even if you aren't completely comfortable with affection, practice being more affectionate with your partner. Make a point to connect physically several times a day. Over time, you'll feel more affectionate and create a deeper emotional bond with your partner.

## 8. You inspire and support each other to be better.

You do this not just in your words but also in your actions. You show your spouse that you want him or her to succeed. You help your partner reach his or her goals and dreams, and you certainly don't undermine a goal that your partner has out of jealously or indifference.

Each person deeply wants the best for the other and lovingly challenges the other to reach his or her full potential. In fact, you see the positive qualities in each other and reflect them back. You don't try to diminish each other or focus on flaws or past mistakes.

## 9. You accept each other for whom you are.

You know this person inside and out. You've seen his or her strengths and weaknesses. You know the personality and behaviors. You see your spouse or partner as an individual worthy of your respect and acceptance—not as a reflection of you or an extension of your ego.

You don't try to change who they are or how they operate in the world. You may request behavior changes or negotiate priorities or decisions, but you never try to control or mold the person into whom you think they should be.

## 10. You like each other.

Solid, healthy relationships are grounded in friendship. You simply like this person you live with. You enjoy the company. You have things to talk about. You laugh together. You make plans together.

You are honestly able to say that not only is this person your lover, life partner, and co-parent—he or she is your best friend.

Remember, it requires both people to be committed to the health of the relationship for it to thrive. And it requires that both people have worked on their emotional baggage, insecurities, and personal growth.

A happy, mutually satisfying relationship is comprised of two people with solid self-esteem, a strong desire to put the relationship first, and the willingness to work through conflict quickly and kindly.

If you are starting over and looking for a new relationship, you need to not only recognize the signs of an emotional abuser, but also look for the traits of someone who is emotionally mature and mentally healthy.

Barrie Davenport

# Conclusion:
# Creating an
# Abuse-Free Future

*"Never be bullied into silence. Never allow yourself to be made a victim. Accept no one's definition of your life; define yourself."*

—Harvey Fierstein

Now that you have reached the end of this book, I hope you have come to the firm decision that emotional abuse is no longer acceptable in your life. I hope your perspective has changed enough to take real action for lasting change.

If you've been doing some of the self-work, meeting with a counselor, and making some of the difficult decisions related to improving your relationship or ending it, the last thing you need is to fall back into the destructive patterns you've lived with for so long. You've come too far for that.

I wish I could tell you that with this new awareness, your life will instantly change, but I think you know that recovery from an abusive relationship is a work in progress. Yes, you CAN heal and move on to a happier life and a healthier relationship, but it takes time, commitment and effort. This effort is well worth it for your future life.

In the past, you may have been an emotional abuse magnet because of your own behavior patterns and past experiences. Now as you've become more empowered and self-aware, you won't find abusive personalities as attractive, and they won't be attracted to the new you—a person who doesn't put up with manipulative, controlling, and hurtful behaviors.

You still need to remain vigilant to ensure you don't fall into an abusive situation again. If you decide to stay with your current partner to work on your relationship or sit in a holding pattern until you're able to leave, these are some things you need to think about:

## Stay alert.

Be on the lookout for the abusive behaviors and words your partner has used in the past, and pay attention to how your partner treats you on a daily basis. Don't allow any old behaviors to slide past you without saying something.

If you allow your partner to revert to his or her old ways, you're sending the message that you're still OK with the abuse. Yes, it may disturb the fragile new peace and equanimity you have recently established, but you can't accept abuse in the name of peace any more. You have to mean business.

## Trust yourself and your judgment.

Your partner spent years trying to undermine your good judgment and make you question yourself. Please don't allow that to happen any more.

If you feel a comment or look is demeaning or sarcastic, it probably is. Don't allow your partner to wriggle out of it by saying, "I'm just kidding." Set up a kind-words-only policy in your home where sarcasm and "joking" at your expense simply aren't allowed.

## Remain clear on your boundaries.

Continue to communicate what you will and won't tolerate from your partner any longer. Have a plan of action for what you'll do or where you will go if those boundaries are crossed. Follow through every single time.

## Continue to communicate your goals.

If you want to work it out with your partner, continue to let him or her know your desire to build an emotionally mature relationship based on love and mutual respect.

Let your spouse know you are committed to therapy and working things out if the abuse can stop. At some point, your spouse may get the message and take you up on it.

## Remember, it's a pattern that counts.

If your partner does want to change, don't breathe a complete sigh of relief until the old pattern of behavior is replaced for a lengthy period of time with a new pattern.

A few instances of good behavior don't merit a pass for bad behavior, even if it's occasional. Slip-ups will happen, but your partner must take full responsibility for them, apologize, and continue to work on changing his or her behavior.

If you have decided to leave your abusive relationship, the best thing you can do for yourself and your ability to heal and become stronger is to take a break from romantic relationships for a while.

Rather than jumping immediately back into a connection with someone, give yourself time to figure out exactly what you want and to rebuild your confidence in yourself. The last thing you want is to attract another abusive partner in your life, and if you're jumping into a new relationship out of fear of being alone, that's exactly who you'll attract.

# Entering a New Relationship

When you decide to date, commit to yourself to take it slowly before getting too deeply involved with a new love interest both sexually and emotionally.

Once you are involved romantically, it becomes much harder to walk away when abusive behaviors start to surface. Women in particular should be aware that having sex with your new romantic interest creates a chemical bond to them, as you release oxytocin in your brain, a bonding agent that makes you fall in love.

You need time to get to know this person and to make sure you aren't repeating the past. As you know, emotional abusers can be charming and persuasive in the beginning, so don't allow yourself to be fooled.

You need enough time to learn about the real person underneath the new relationship shininess that people project. Only time will allow you to see the authentic person and how he or she behaves and reacts in different situations.

Also, be aware you aren't simply looking for someone to take care of you or fulfill an area of neediness. You may again attract someone who is critical and controlling or someone to rescue you. You want a partnership based on equality, respect, and love.

That's why it's so important to take the time to get stronger and more self-assured—so that you are someone a confident, self-assured partner will be attracted to.

When you're beginning a new romance and hopeful it will work out, you may not want to constantly assess the behavior of this new person for any warning signs. You just want to enjoy the thrill of this wonderful connection. But it's especially important that you remain aware of the possibility of re-entering an abusive situation before you get too involved with any new partner.

Here are some behaviors you want to be on the lookout for:

- Poor impulse control

- Low self-esteem

- Selfishness and narcissism

- Needy and demanding behaviors

- Alcohol or drug abuse

- A past history of abuse

- A history of mental illness

- Inability to support himself or herself financially or emotionally

- Personality disorder

- Antisocial behavior

- Aggressiveness

- Needing to feel powerful and in control

- Being preoccupied with sex and wanting it daily or many times a day

- Poor social skills

As a new relationship matures, it's important that you have a candid conversation with your love interest to discuss your expectations of each other. If you feel safe discussing your previous relationship, let this new person know about the emotional abuse and how strongly you feel about not repeating this pattern.

Discuss your personal boundaries and talk about the kind of relationship you're hoping to build with a new person—one that doesn't involve control, manipulation, and fear.

Be specific and clear about behaviors you won't tolerate, and listen closely to this new person's expectations. You'll be much happier you had this conversation, even if it becomes clear this isn't the person for you.

When you do find a new love who treats you with kindness and respect, you'll need to continue setting boundaries and monitoring your own tendencies toward losing yourself within the relationship. Continue to work on being an independent person with your own friends, interests, and activities.

Pay attention to any tendency you might have to give up what you really want to keep peace or accommodate your partner—or to avoid making decisions and be responsible for yourself.

You are looking for an equal relationship in which neither of you is viewed as "better than" the other. You definitely don't want a relationship where you feel less accomplished, intelligent, attractive, or powerful.

If you enter a "less than" relationship, you will give away your power and set the tone for a potentially abusive situation.

As a result of living through an abusive relationship, some former victims have a hard time opening their hearts to a new person. Your own "abuse radar" may sit on high alert all the time, making it difficult to see the real person you are dating, because you're constantly scanning for bad behavior.

You will have to learn to trust again and recognize what a healthy relationship really is. You may feel so wounded that you misinterpret acceptable behavior and push away someone who is well-meaning and authentic.

It may be difficult for you to accept genuine love, because you are so accustomed to receiving only crumbs. Feeling real love from someone might be overwhelming and even painful, because it reminds you of all the times you didn't receive the love you craved.

This pain and confusion is part of the healing process, and you must allow yourself to open up to receive love and let it fill the emptiness inside you. Over time, you will learn to trust again and enjoy the richness of an intimate and loving connection with someone new.

I want to thank you so much for reading this book and for having the courage to address the emotional abuse in your life. I know it's painful and challenging, but knowledge brings you power, and now you have more knowledge about your situation and what you need to do.

Every small step you take toward ending the abuse in your life and reclaiming your personal power is an act of self-love. You ARE deserving of a happy, loving, intimate, respectful, peaceful, and fear-free relationship. Accept nothing less.

I hope you'll visit my site, Live Bold and Bloom.com, for more practical articles and information giving you strategies for living a confident, authentic life. Also, I'd love to hear your feedback about this book and how it's impacted your situation. Please feel free to email me at mybloomlife@gmail.com.

Barrie Davenport

# List of Emotionally Abusive Patterns and Behaviors

## Domination

Showing boredom when you talk, using crossed arms, head down, deep sighs.

Saying things to upset or frighten you.

Making you do humiliating or demeaning things.

Giving you disapproving or contemptuous looks or body language.

Viewing you as an extension of himself or herself, rather than an individual.

Monitoring your time and whereabouts.

Monitoring your telephone calls or email contacts.

Making decisions that affect both of you or the family without consulting you or reaching agreement with you.

Withholding resources, such as money.

Restricting your usage of the telephone and/or car.

Not allowing you to leave the home alone.

Preventing you from working or attending school.

Preventing you from socializing with friends and/or seeing his or her family.

Preventing you from seeking medical care or other types of help.

## Verbal Assaults

Yelling at you.

Insulting you.

Using sarcasm or "teasing" to put you down or make you feel bad.

Swearing at you or calling you names.

Belittling, insulting, or ridiculing you.

Mimicking, invalidating, or patronizing you.

## Demanding Expectations

Expecting you to talk to him or her, while you're watching TV, reading, or game playing.

Ordering you around/treating you like a servant.

Demanding obedience to whims.

Not tolerating any seeming lack of respect.

Refusing to share in housework or childcare.

Having an inability to laugh at himself or herself and not tolerating you or others laughing at them.

## Emotional Blackmail

Escalating abusive language or behavior if you talk back.

Using guilt trips or shaming to get his or her way.

Withholding sex or affection to get his or her way.

Being frequently emotionally distant or emotionally unavailable.

Becoming angry or cold when chores are not done when wanted or as wanted.

Using neglect or abandonment to punish or frighten you.

Threatening to leave the relationship.

Acting indifferently to your feelings.

Showing a general lack of empathy and compassion.

Threatening suicide if you leave.

## Unpredictable Behavior

Having unpredictable emotional outbursts.

Stomping out of a room during an argument or heated discussion.

Sulking and refusing to talk about an issue.

Giving the silent treatment.

Throwing objects (but not at you).

Hitting or kicking a wall, furniture, doors, etc.

Shaking a finger or fist at you.

Making threatening gestures or faces.

Threatening to destroy or destroying personal property that belongs to you.

Threatening to use physical or sexual aggression against you.

Driving dangerously while you're in the car as a conscious intentional act to scare or intimidate.

Using your children to threaten you (for example, threatening to kidnap the children).

Threatening violence against your children, family, friends, or pets.

## Chaos and Crisis Creation

Acting jealous and suspicious of your friends and social contacts.

Repeatedly crossing your boundaries and ignoring requests.

Blaming you for life difficulties, problems, or unhappiness.

Doing something to spite you.

Intentionally starting arguments.

Compulsively lying.

Intentionally attacking or demeaning things or people important to you.

Pouting or acting dramatic to get attention.

Getting inappropriately hysterical.

Threatening to harm himself or herself.

## Character Assassination

Belittling, insulting, or berating you in front of other people.

Putting down your physical appearance or intellect.

Correcting or chastising you for your behavior.

Belittling and trivializing you, your accomplishments, or your hopes and dreams.

Regularly pointing out your flaws, mistakes, or shortcomings.

Sharing personal information about you with others.

Putting down your friends and/or family.

Telling you your feelings are irrational or crazy.

Turning other people against you.

## Gaslighting

Accusing you of being "too sensitive" to deflect his or her abusive remarks.

Using deceptive communication.

Playing intentional mind games.

Blaming you for his or her bad behavior.

Accusing or blaming you of things that aren't true, such as infidelity.

Invalidating or denying his or her emotionally abusive behavior when confronted.

## Sexual Harassment

Trying to shame or cajole you into having sex.

Pushing you into sexual acts you don't feel comfortable with.

Insults or demeans you sexually.

Threatens to have affairs if you don't have sex.

Barrie Davenport

# Support Resources

Emotional Abuse Breakthrough Course
(http://emotionallyabused.com/)

Find a Therapist
(https://therapists.psychologytoday.com/rms/)

Breakthrough Behavioral, Inc. online therapy
(https://www.breakthrough.com/)

HelpGuide.org, resource for mental, emotional, and
social health
(http://www.helpguide.org/)

WomensHealth.gov
(http://womenshealth.gov/)

Facebook Emotional Abuse Awareness
support group
(https://www.facebook.com/groups/18628385831/?f
ref=ts)

Facebook Emotional Abuse support group
(https://www.facebook.com/groups/2863330782000
34/?fref=ts)

Barrie Davenport

The National Domestic Violence Hotline
1-800-799-SAFE (7233)
1-800-787-3224 (TTY)
(http://www.thehotline.org/)

Childhelp National Child Abuse Hotline
1-800-4-A-CHILD (1-800-442-4453)
(https://www.childhelp.org/hotline/)

## Sources for Citations

### Introduction

Diane Follingstad.
See http://uknowledge.uky.edu/crvaw_facpub/83/

### Chapter 1

Andrew Vachss.
See http://www.vachss.com/av_dispatches/disp_9408_a.html

George Simon.
See http://www.manipulative-people.com/covert-
aggressives-manipulative-wolves-in-sheeps-clothing/

### Chapter 2

University of Oregon Study.
See http://pages.uoregon.edu/dynamic/jjf/theses/goldsmith04.htm

### Chapter 4

Study of Spanish students.
See http://www.psicothema.com/psicothema.asp?id=3334

## Chapter 5

Sam Vaknin.
See http://samvak.tripod.com/abusefamily.html

Abusive Men.
See https://en.wikipedia.org/wiki/Psychological_abuse

Sam Vaknin.
See http://samvak.tripod.com/abusefamily2.html

## Chapter 6

Michael Formica.
See https://www.psychologytoday.com/blog/enlightened-living/200807/understanding-the-dynamics-abusive-relationships

## Chapter 11

George Simon.
Seehttp://counsellingresource.com/features/2009/05/14/empowerment-tools-recognizing-defining-and-respecting-boundaries/

## Chapter 17

Tara Palmatier.
See http://shrink4men.com/2013/04/30/obsessing-over-an-abusive-ex-thoughts-on-being-stuck/

## Chapter 20

Stan Tatkin, *Wired for Love: How Understanding Your Partner's Brain and Attachment Style Can Help You Defuse Conflict and Build a Secure Relationship*, New Harbinger Publication, 2012.

Barrie Davenport

# Want to Learn More?

If you'd like to learn more about emotional abuse, healthy relationships, confidence, and self-esteem, please visit my blog, Live Bold and Bloom.com http://liveboldandbloom.com/, and check out my course, Emotional Abuse Breakthrough http://emotionallyabused.com/.

Barrie Davenport

# Did You Like *Emotional Abuse Breakthrough?*

Thank you so much for purchasing *Emotional Abuse Breakthrough: How to Speak Up, Set Boundaries, and Break the Cycle of Manipulation and Control with Your Abusive Partner.* I'm honored by the trust you've placed in me and my work by choosing this book to better understand emotional abuse and try to end it in your relationship. I truly hope you've enjoyed it and found it useful for your life.

I'd like to ask you for a small favor. Would you please take just a minute to leave a review for this book on Amazon? This feedback will help me continue to write the kind of books that will best serve you. If you really loved the book, please let me know!

Barrie Davenport

# Other Books You Might Enjoy from Barrie Davenport

*Building Confidence: Get Motivated, Overcome Social Fear, Be Assertive, and Empower Your Life for Success* (liveboldandbloom.com/building-confidence)

*Peace of Mindfulness: Everyday Rituals to Conquer Anxiety and Claim Unlimited Inner Peace* (liveboldandbloom.com/mindfulness-post)

*Finely Tuned: How to Thrive as a Highly Sensitive Person or Empath* (liveboldandbloom.com/finely-tuned)

*201 Relationship Questions: The Couple's Guide to Building Trust and Emotional Intimacy* (liveboldandbloom.com/201-questions)

*Self-Discovery Questions: 155 Breakthrough Questions to Accelerate Massive Action* (liveboldandbloom.com/questions-book)

*Confidence Hacks: 99 Small Actions to Massively Boost Your Confidence* (liveboldandbloom.com/confidence-hacks)

*10-Minute Declutter: The Stress-Free Habit for Simplifying Your Home* (liveboldandbloom.com/10-min-declutter)

*10-Minute Digital Declutter: The Simple Habit to Eliminate Technology Overload* (liveboldandbloom.com/digital-declutter)

*Declutter Your Mind: How to Stop Worrying, Relieve Anxiety, and Eliminate Negative Thinking* (liveboldandbloom.com/declutter-mind)

*Sticky Habits: 6 Simple Steps to Create Good Habits That Stick* (liveboldandbloom.com/habitbook)

*The 52-Week Life Passion Project: Uncover Your Life Passion* (liveboldandbloom.com/life-passion-book)

Made in the USA
Lexington, KY
26 July 2017